THE RELUCTANT NATURALIST

A Study of G.E. Moore's *Principia Ethica*

Dennis Rohatyn

Professor of Philosophy
University of San Diego
Alcala Park
San Diego, California 92110

UNIVERSITY
PRESS OF
AMERICA

LANHAM • NEW YORK • LONDON

Copyright © 1987 by

University Press of America,® Inc.

4720 Boston Way
Lanham, MD 20706

3 Henrietta Street
London WC2E 8LU England

All rights reserved

Printed in the United States of America

British Cataloging in Publication Information Available

Library of Congress Cataloging in Publication Data

Rohatyn, Dennis A.
The reluctant naturalist.

Bibliography: p.
1. Moore, G. E. (George Edward), 1873-1958.
Principia ethica.   2. Ethics.   I. Title.
B1647.M73P7537   1987   171'.2   86-26637
ISBN 0-8191-5767-8 (alk. paper)
ISBN 0-8191-5768-6 (pbk. : alk. paper)

B
1647
.M73
P7537
1987

All University Press of America books are produced on acid-free
paper which exceeds the minimum standards set by the National
Historical Publication and Records Commission.

For my daughters

ABSTRACT

This study has two principal aims. One is to discredit the fact/value dichotomy by showing it to be logically absurd. The other is to offer a new interpretation of G.E. Moore's contribution to value-theory, which assists in reaching the first goal. We give a number of arguments intended to prove that the f/v dichotomy is self-refuting. We present 20 separate formulations of Moore's naturalistic fallacy, unifying them as diverse corollaries of the open-question argument. We examine the principle of organic unities as a restatement of the naturalistic fallacy, as showing Moore's partial break with the tenets of absolute idealism, and as anticipating the novel aesthetic doctrines encountered in the last chapter of <u>Principia Ethica</u>. A review of the isolation test of value, the several criteria for beauty and the attack on theodicies discloses that Moore's specific insights about intrinsic value undermine his own purported non-naturalism. We discuss some of Moore's commentators, and treat a number of philosophers whose views on fact and value resemble or concur with our own. We conclude by meeting logical objections to the positions we maintain, while showing the bearing of Moore's work on ultimate human concerns.

PREFACE

This book is not a commentary on all of Moore's works, and it is not a treatise on values. It is something of a cross between the two, very selective in its emphasis and confined to a few topics that the author happens to favor. I have kept a promise to myself, not to comment on the supposed relation between 'good' and the color yellow, or the 143 types of definition, 142 of which Moore did not acknowledge. These are dead-end topics. Moore is hard enough to stomach without a nauseating and by this time superfluous review of the weakest points in his writings. So I chose instead to indulge myself, and spare the reader in the bargain. I have structured the book around the problem of fact vs. value. Those and only those issues which I find exciting, stimulating or of undeniable relevance to Moore and to the future of value-theory as a discipline are included.

Did I say I chose? I am not sufficiently skillful, or enough of a sophist, to plead determinism as an excuse, both for sins of omission and of commission. The book expresses my interests, and it is written exactly the way I felt it had to be. Does any author ever think otherwise? Beyond that, I make no defense of its contents. It may say something important, or be a tissue of nonsense; conceivably, both. George Orwell, who was born in the same year (1903) as <u>Principia Ethica</u> appeared, said in 1946 that every book is a failure, including the novel (<u>1984</u>) he was then planning. I wish I could fail as well and as memorably as did Orwell. My only hope is not to become complacent at the level of non-fictional mediocrity I attain.

I owe three major debts of gratitude. The first is to Abraham Edel, who introduced me to ethics and to Moore simultaneously. From Edel I learned not to discount Moore prematurely, and to give the text every benefit of scholarly doubt, no matter how snarled or hopeless the writing and reasoning appeared to be. Whether I have learned anything else, only he could say. The second is to Elmer Klemke, who got me interested in (and excited about) writing on Moore, and caught me up in his enthusiasm for Moore scholarship in general. Klemke found time both to encourage and to prod my work. He is also ultimately responsible for my continued fascination with Moore, over the last decade. The third is to Tom Regan, delightful colleague and co-founder of the G.E. Moore Society. Thanks to Regan's diligent research, Moore's early (pre-1903) period is finally due for its own renascence, after decades of neglect. Moore's permanent legacy owes much to those years, and we owe much to Regan for recovering them.

I am also grateful to John Crosby for his oral and written comments on a paper I gave at Houston in 1982; these stimulated me to rethink Moore, to dig into the relevant texts and sharpen the presentation at crucial stages. My students in Philosophy 155 indulged my addiction to Moore, and forgave my tortured exposition of his thought for several years. The publisher's referee was generous in praise and acute in criticism; I benefited greatly from both. The publisher tolerated my delays in revising the typescript with unusual grace. University of San Diego made life pleasant, by granting a six-month sabbatical to complete this book, and unlimited use of their computer facilities, on holidays and weekends. My colleagues' queries ("How's it coming along?") spurred me to finish before other obligations overwhelmed me. I appreciate all the help, both tangible and intangible.

Naomi, you said I would turn into a prune if I kept going back and forth to school. You were right. Heather, "TV nose" is coming home at last. I love you both so so so so so so much.

TABLE OF CONTENTS

	Page
ABSTRACT.	iv
PREFACE	v

Chapters

I	The Place of Fact in a World of Value .	1
II	A Disputation (Objections A-H).	4
III	Antecedents	11
IV	The Textbook Moore.	19
V	A Guided Tour of *Principia Ethica* (PE), Chapter I	20

    A. The Naturalistic Fallacy (NF) . . . 20
    B. The Principle of Organic Unities
       (POU) 34

VI	Intermezzo: Ontology and Value.	38
VII	A Second Tour: *Principia Ethica* (PE), Chapter VI.	55

    Round 1: The Real vs. the Not So Real. 55
    Round 2: Possible Worlds vs. Actual
              Agents. 61
    Round 3: And Still a Fallacy!. 67
    Round 4: Knowledge and Beauty. 69
    Round 5: What Hath Moore Wrought?. . . 72
    Round 6: A Thing of Beauty is a
              Thing Forever 74

VIII	The Autopsy of Fact/Value	83

    A. Tidying Up. 83
    B. Pluralism and Its Problems. 86

IX	Exorcising Intrinsic Value.	94

    A. The Evidence. 94
    B. The Dilemma 97
    C. The Solution. 98

| X | Facing the Values . . . . 107 |

    1. Preamble. 107
    2. Meeting the Opposition Half-Way . . 107
    3. Whose Fallacy?. 110
    4. Is Denial of the Fact/Value
       Dichotomy Self-Refuting?. 115
    5. The Frankfurt Connection. 120
    6. Life-Boat Axiology. 128
    7. Coda. 129

REFERENCES AND WORKS CONSULTED. 131

CHAPTER I

THE PLACE OF FACT IN A WORLD OF VALUE

I begin with some deceptively simple questions: (1) What is a fact? (2) What is a value? (3) What do we mean by the fact/value dichotomy? (4) What is the relation between fact and value? and (5) Why are we bothering to investigate this problem?

My not so simple answers are as follows:

(1) A fact is some state of affairs which an agent singles out for attention. Not every state of affairs is a fact, but only those of which a person or community is or chooses to be aware, at a given time.

(2) A value is the object of some desire, choice, or preference. It designates properties, qualities or relationships in virtue of which one undertakes action for the sake of some end. It can (sometimes) be measured in terms of the sacrifices one is prepared to make or the things one is ready to relinquish in order to obtain or secure the end in question.

(3) We don't mean anything by it. Once upon a time, philosophers alleged that 'facts' and 'values' were mutually exclusive categories. Hence, from a set of stated facts, no matter how complete and how proper, it was held impossible ever to infer or deduce any conclusion involving value. If only facts appeared in the premises of an argument, then only facts could legitimately be inferred in the conclusion. Conversely, if a conclusion contained a value-term, then at least one value-term must have appeared in at least one of the preceding premises. This injunction was known as the fact/value "gap," as Hume's "fork" between 'is' and 'ought' propositions, and by various other names.

We can see from (1) and (2) that a fact/value dichotomy is bogus. Since both facts and values require choices, they have something in common and cannot be treated as mutually exclusive. Moreover, the selection of a fact as something worthy of attention depends upon making an evaluation. The majority of states of affairs go unnoticed, no matter how many World Almanacs we compile. Hence, it is no exaggeration to say that facts presuppose values. This remark does not imply that we can "derive" an 'is' from an 'ought,' since the term 'presuppose' has a different meaning from 'entail.' But it does shift the burden of proof. For a long time, philosophers were wont to maintain that facts along were "objective," whereas values were unavoidably "subjective." Thanks to the invalidity of the f/v disjunction, we can see that this position is false. Either facts are as "subjective' as values, or else values are (in general) as "objective" as facts. Whether the distinction between subjective and objective can be redrawn on other grounds is beside the point; even if it can, this lends no support to an invidious discrimination between values and facts, and cannot be based on the latter, either.

(4) Since facts presuppose values, it is correct to include facts within the domain of value. That explains, among other things, the title of this chapter. Since facts are a special type of value, it remains correct to distinguish the two, much as we identify elephants within the larger class of mammals. A distinction is not a dichotomy, and it does not license the sort of moves which proponents of the is/ought and other "distinctions" are prone to make. The invariable failure of attempts to erect a f/v gap is not due to human frailty, but to the groundlessness of the disjunction.

(5) The position taken above is bound to seem counter-intuitive. We are accustomed to using language in ways that reinforce a f/v gap rather than its denial. We have been trained to present philosophical and other problems which rely on making, rather than challenging, just such a contrast. It is natural for us to think immediately of everything that must be mistaken, or at least suspect, about paragraphs (3) and (4). I want to anticipate, and respond to, such objections right away. Before I can do so, I must explain my own intentions. My subject is G.E. Moore. Moore's famous "naturalistic fallacy" did more to boost the reputation of the f/v dichotomy than any technique before or since. Today we know that the naturalistic fallacy is questionable, yet we have not quite overcome its influence. This book offers a reinterpretation, not just of the fallacy, but of Moore's thought on value and value-theory, as a whole. But before we can examine Moore, we need to

understand our own situation, eight decades after the publication of <u>Principia Ethica</u> (1903). This is why I began the analysis by refuting the f/v dichotomy, independently of any reference to Moore. So you know where I stand, or fall. My next task is to cure the reader of any lingering doubts or skepticism, by examining as many rebuttals to my own position as possible. Doing so will also enable me to draw on portions of the recent literature. This in turn will help to disclose where some of our most distinguished contemporaries find themselves in the struggle to overcome entrenched conventions and to arrive at some new and more refined insights concerning the relation between fact and value.

CHAPTER II

A DISPUTATION (OBJECTIONS A-H)

Objection A. "The word 'fact'...is treacherous, involving the old confusion between the actual situation and the description of it" [Hampshire (1949), repr. in (1971), 55n5]. Your claim that facts presuppose values simply conflates the facts themselves with what it is to "analyze and interpret" them.

I reply that I do no such thing. Facts are a subset of states of affairs. The latter are what the objection refers to as "facts themselves." This is why I took the pains to say at the outset that not every state of affairs is a fact, but only those to which individuals or institutions may call their own or others' attention, at a given moment. A fact is a social phenomenon. Hence, I find it misleading to speak of "facts themselves," even though we use this expression with perfect propriety in everyday life. (Of course, there can be facts about facts, as in sociology, but this is another story.) Granted, everyone is entitled to define terms as they see fit, provided no radical incoherence or contradiction results from it. Can we extend the same courtesy to my definition of 'fact'? We can, indeed we must. For if we don't, then the f/v distinction collapses into the uninteresting distinction between states of affairs (the colloquial "facts themselves") and values. Uninteresting, and even untrue. For (the existence of) values is surely a state of affairs in its own right. If we can quantify over value-predicates, then, since 'to be is to be a value of a variable,' to be a value is to be a value of a variable, too. How can the pretensions of maintaining a f/v cleavage be kept up under those circumstances?

This discussion shows that we largely take the notion of fact for granted in dealing with the relation between fact and value. This already places an unfair burden on the latter concept, and tends to prejudice the outcome of analysis in advance.

Objection B. If what you say in reply to A. is correct, then Dewey was right to hold that there is no difference between value propositions and potato propositions [Dewey (1939), 19]. But surely there is all the difference in the world. Potatoes have all sorts of observable properties; notoriously, values do not. Doesn't your line of argument run contrary to that?

I reply that if values are intangible, so is pi, or the square root of 2. States of affairs may be as Platonic (or as materialistic) as you like.Overcoming the antithesis between fact and value does not compel us to adopt (or reject) any given ontology. Besides, there Dewey was discussing propositions, not entities or events. True (and false) propositions have things in common, regardless of subject.Language is part of the world, but it is also distinguishable from what it describes. Otherwise, we are again liable to be misled by phrases such as "the facts themselves."

Objection C has two variants:

C1. Your definition of 'fact' does assume that reality is something independent from what we can conceive or imagine. It is therefore unacceptable to (e.g.) a Berkeleyan idealist. It is therefore disingenuous to argue that ontology has no bearing on the dissolution of the f/v dichotomy.

I reply that if we do <u>not</u> distinguish between facts and the states of affairs in which they are included, then the f/v dichotomy collapses immediately. Since every claim about reality is in that case reducible to the report of an experience or a mental episode, value claims will simply be part of one's individual (or collective) phenomenology (or history), like everything else. This does not mean that there would be no criteria by which to assess whether experience was veridical or internally coherent. To rescue objectivity, an idealist may posit God (as Berkeley did), or else fall back upon scientific tests and predictions as a way of gauging the trustworthiness of appearances. An idealist is not committed to regarding hypotheses as either incorrigible or infallible. But (s)he has no good reason for excluding values from this process of validation or verification, since their status is continuous with experience in general, and is therefore subject to the same method of ratification. An idealist cannot help but be a naturalist.

Consequently, the assumption that states of affairs exist independently of their social discovery is a generous one. In its absence, the fiction of a f/v dichotomy cannot be maintained for longer than an instant. There is nonetheless an irony surrounding this form of protest, since, if it were valid, the objector would be forced to concede the relevance of fact (ontology) for the determination of value.

C2. The objection may mean something entirely different from the preceding. We argue for several theses in this book. Every argument presupposes a distinction between what its proponent regards as true and as false, respectively. Doesn't this show that (respect for) objectivity is logically anterior to our attempt to abolish it, and therefore, that the denial of the f/v dichotomy is self-contradictory?

There are several answers to this. (a) Truth and falsity are both norms of inquiry. Hence, the presupposition in question supports the very argument we are making. (b) Respect for objectivity is also a norm, and argues the same case on our behalf. (c) The denial of the f/v dichotomy is not an attempt to abolish objectivity; quite the contrary. We are merely so used to thinking of facts as "objective," values as "subjective" that any argument against that appears counter-intuitive. (d) Objectivity in the sense of (belief in) the existence of a world that is (in part) unconditioned by human thought and activity is in no way disturbed by the denial of the f/v split, for reasons already given in response to objection C1. (For more on how "objectivity" is compatible with the position taken in this book, see Chapter X, pp. 107-110.)

Objection D. Since you define 'fact' as something which we "single out for attention," and 'value' as the object of "desire, choice, or pref-erence," it is no surprise that you conclude that fact and value are interrelated. By rigging the definitions in your favor, the result is guaranteed.

I reply that (i) as replies to preceding objectives show, alternative definitions of 'fact' are either muddled or else lead to the same result.

(ii) My definition of 'fact' follows Dewey in looking at the world from the standpoint of an organism which is attempting to gain (or restore) equilibrium with its environment. This frankly Darwinian approach enables us to understand why creatures cannot afford to treat states of affairs indifferently. Some things are more important to us (in given contexts, for certain purposes) than others. Survival (both individual and species) dictates selection as well as exclusion of data. These remarks are subject to additional qualifications. Some facets of attention are genetically programmed, rather than overtly decided upon. Some are subject to modification in light of experience. We may regret an action or omission, and may seek to redirect our behavior, accordingly. But some habits are harder to break than others. Try as we might, we cannot hear high-pitched sounds, even though we can invent instruments capable of making (and detecting) them. We may perish as a consequence of ignoring something; that is an extreme case of learning the hard way. Our (collective) criteria for what is worth paying attention to are not static, but grow as a function of time and trial. Indeed, they must. Even the goals are not fixed or frozen; an individual (or community) may opt for death, or transcend its original conception of ends and means. And so on.

(iii) The nuances of what the term 'fact' connotes are of course open to debate; the initial formulation was kept succinct, to avoid undue complications. The intention throughout is to strengthen our understanding of a concept which the tradition has neglected, or else regarded as self-evident. This illustrates the very dangers inherent in the process of selection and exclusion, mentioned above. Fortunately, once a fact becomes a fact, errors made in prior ignorance of it become avoidable, as self-correction takes place.

(iv) We are in no position to judge the force of the "begged question" objection until we have expounded Moore's famous 'open question' argument. Then we will see just what it amounts to, and how it can be met.

Objection E. Your definition of 'fact' may be in order, but your definition of 'value' is arbitrary. Hence, the collapse of the f/v distinction is still merely a function of your choice of vocabulary.

I reply that (i) there are at least 35 extant definitions of 'value' available in current scholarly literature [Baier, in Baier and Rescher (1969), 35-36n]. My definition distills three recurrent features of prior explications: value as that which

is prized or cherished, value as the basis for
ranking of ends and for rational performance in
accordance with such ranking, and value as a quantity
(of energy, time or money) expended in exchange for
something sought. There may be other points
deserving scrutiny, but these will do as a beginning.
(ii) Another definition may be substituted, provided
it furthers discussion of relevant issues. But
definitions can become the source of false hopes.
For example, Baier defines 'value' as a thing's
"...capacity to confer a benefit on someone, to make
a favorable difference to his life" [Baier, 40]. He
further defines what it is for a person (S) to hold a
given value (V) as follows: "1) V vaguely points to
or indicates possible states of affairs, 2) towards
whose realization S has a favorable attitude, and 3)
because S believes, explicitly or implicitly, that
their realization makes a favorable difference to the
life of someone, not necessarily S himself" [Baier,
57]. The reader may inspect this and gauge its
consequences for our present discussion. Without
going into details, I submit that Baier's approach
allows fact to collide with value, instantly. This
is not a reproach. No definition of either of these
terms can succeed in keeping them separate for long,
unless it _is_ arbitrary, or else based on a
"metaphysical thesis" which demands holding them
apart [cf. Searle (1969), 198]. While my
formulations are not idiosyncratic, one is always
free to reject them and try something different. But
it would be naive to suppose that opposition to the
f/v dichotomy is merely the product of clever (or
disguised) linguistic arrangements. It may be nearer
the truth to say this of the f/v dichotomy itself.

    Objection F. Values "supervene" on facts. They
are never part of the data; they are always an
additional judgment, interpretation, or construction
placed on the data.

    I reply that, this is also true of
Schroedinger's wave amplitude equation (in quantum
mechanics), when considered apart from its
eigenfunctions. It is true of all "theory-laden"
observations, in or out of science. It is even true
of human communication, insofar as we conceive of it
as creating a universe of meaning, whose symbol
systems express the ability to transcend our own
space-time environment. Of course, this is another
way of denying that there are ever "just facts"--the
very phrase is obliquely self-contradictory. To be a

fact is to be a matter of concern which goes beyond mere presence or reportage. This has nothing to do with bias, distortion, or problems allied with reliable ascertainment of facts, which notion likewise presupposes certain values. Insofar as there is always (and necessarily) something more than "fact" operative in the human interventions which aim to disclose states of affairs, nothing about that phenomenon is unique, strange, or confined to a given set of situations. It may even turn out that facts and values can be ontologically assimilated to one another [cf. pp. 126-127], in which case the claim that values "supervene" on facts is neither necessary nor sufficient for characterizing anything [cf. Rohatyn (1976), 95-100].

Objection G. If the f/v disjunction is abandoned, aren't we simply giving in to relativism? Aren't we in effect saying that one person's values are as good (or right) as another's?

I reply that, this hardly follows. On the contrary, with the exception of Kant it is exceedingly difficult to avoid relativism once a f/v disjunction is admitted. Once the "autonomy of ethics" is mandated, value terms must justify themselves; no extra-disciplinary vindication is allowed. Small wonder that Kant chose a rule-governed approach, or that he insisted on the a priori character of the categorical imperative. If scientific or anthropological findings were outlawed, one could go them one better by producing a quasi-mathematical theorem of value. But if that approach also failed, one would be in the same predicament as Euthyphro, whose explications of 'piety' were unavoidably circular. If facts are "hard" whereas values are "soft," then bridging the f/v gap needn't make facts soft (for an interesting look at how politics and technology underlie the evolution of "hard fact" as a criterion for responsible mass media journalism, see Smith (1978), 143-149, 193-198). Instead, it may succeed in making values hard, as though hardness were desirable (not to mention the sexual innuendos lurking here). The point is that dismissal of the f/v split can work to the advantage of both, rather than to the detriment of either. Dewey's emphasis on the difference between the 'satisfying' and the 'satisfactory' [Dewey (1939), 5,32] speaks directly to this issue.

Objection H. We can agree that means-ends relationships (like Kant's hypothetical imperatives) are corroborable and can be well-attested. But what about ultimate values? Wasn't Max Weber right [Weber (1949), 55, 57, 110-112] to protest against confusing faith with facts, ideals with testable hypotheses, posits "in which the meaning of our existence is rooted" with the truths "which empirical knowledge along is able to give us?" Isn't any attempted reduction of values to facts phony, pseudo-scientific? Doesn't respect for intellectual integrity demand a f/v dichotomy, for this reason alone?

I reply that, "intellectual integrity" is itself a value. When we are told that the f/v dichotomy is true, we are being asked to adopt a norm of intellectual honesty, hence, one of conduct. Such norms are logically prior to the contexts in which they are invoked. This self-referential paradox is the best proof conceivable that facts do presuppose values. Weber himself (inadvertently) gives this away as soon as he admits that science itself is based on a definite presupposition--the value of (inquiring after) truth. No wonder that "Weber's critics... noticed that the argument for the impossibility of a quasi-deductively 'justified' ethics could not be limited to ethics, but applied as readily to the 'justification' of science, of ontology, and to the distinction between science and ethics itself..." [Turner and Factor (1984), 232]. Some minimal commitment to values is unavoidable, unless we renounce rationality. And renouncing rationality is itself "value-loaded" (as in Kierkegaard's case) thus, quasi-rational. That should tell us something about the inescapability of these conclusions.

To make science "value-free" is neither possible nor desirable. This is gradually being recognized [cf. Hollinger (1975)]. The conclusion that the f/v dichotomy is false or indefensible is likewise dependent on a logically prior norm; but since that argument is based on express acknowledgement of the norm's priority, it is perfectly consistent with its own premises.

I will say much more about "ultimate value" when we are further into Moore. Next, let us look at what some recent philosophers have had to say about the issues just raised, especially in reply to Objection H.

CHAPTER III

ANTECEDENTS

Challenges to the f/v dichotomy have been around for a number of years. Dewey's opposition predates World War II. Searle's famous derivation of 'ought' from 'is' [Searle (1969), 1975 ff.] generated its own secondary literature [cf. Rohatyn (1976), Chapter IV]. Hampshire, writing during the dark age of logical positivism, vigorously rebutted the presumption that unless moral judgments can be mathematically deduced from fact, they "...must be ultimate and irrational, ...established by intuition...not literally significant" [Hampshire (1949), repr. in (1971), 63]. There are undoubtedly other predecessors; omissions should not be taken as slights. Historically the pioneer is C.I. Lewis. Lewis saw more clearly and earlier than anyone else that the denial of cognitive status to all values is logically self-defeating, and he lost no time in communicating this insight. Moore grasped this too, but he conveyed his position ackwardly, without rhetorical punch. Lewis was crisp, but too absorbed with technique [cf. Levi (1974), 198] to make an immediate or lasting impact. So we will begin by looking at several recent formulations which are significant in their own right, and more accessible than those of the masters. After turning to Lewis we will be prepared to deal with Moore.

In _Philosophical Explanations_, Robert Nozick states the following tentative hypothesis: "Values enter into the very definition of what a fact is; the realm of facts cannot be defined or specified without utilizing certain values" [Nozick (1981), 535]. The strongest case for this claim comes from the least expected quarter: science. The sciences cannot operate without certain tacit value commitments, a fact (sic) which Dewey stressed repeatedly throughout his career. As Shrader-Frechette says, "...it is in principle impossible for any scholarly pursuits, even pure science, to avoid constitutive values," or "adherence to values underlying particular rules of scientific method" [Shrader-Frechette (1985), 69, ital. in orig.]. Nozick [(1981) 741 n111] cites Hilary Putnam's forthright exposure of the myth of value neutrality. Putnam argues strenuously that facts presuppose values: "...the view that rational acceptability itself is simply subjective is a self-refuting one....There is no neutral conception of rationality to which to appeal...(however) if there is no conception of rationality one objectively ought to have, then the notion of a 'fact' is empty. Without the cognitive values of coherence, simplicity and instrumental efficacy, we have no world and no 'facts'...(consequently) the argument that there can't be any objective values at all has been refuted" [Putnam (1981), 135-136, 143, italics and single-quotes in original, parentheticals added].

Does Putnam's reductio succeed? Not according to Robert Neville, who contends that "the most the argument proves...is that scientists believe in--or function as if they believe in--the values of inquiry" [Neville (1981), 98]. This amounts to "...what Kant disparaged as a hypothetical justification for the value of inquiry" [Ibidem]. But even that would be enough to cause the opposition acute discomfort. If I manage to prove that inquiry depends upon certain norms, that scientists cannot get along without these norms, that whoever wants to pursue science must employ or invoke them, that scientific activity is impossible unless we accept such norms, then the cost of eschewing norms altogether is to abandon science. Who will pay that price? Not even a Luddite, who dearly wishes to redirect inquiry, not to destroy it. Neville (or a hardened skeptic) might reply that alleged unwillingness to pay the price is merely an ad hominem consideration (though there is evidence that philosophy exists and is founded exclusively on ad hominem arguments [Johnstone (1959)]. Besides, is "eschewing norms altogether" possible, in principle? If so, in the name of what? Value freedom? That, as we saw in Chapter II, is another norm. Hence, anyone who won't pay the price will end up paying double. Withdrawal (and/or suicide) is the sole alternative left. And that is why Putnam's reductio argument is unconditionally valid. Likewise, since "...the science component is not separable from the political/ ethical/evaluative component of technology-related controversies" [Shrader-Frechette (1985), 313], we must guard against "the presupposition that objectivity = neutrality" [Ibid., 81] which fosters the illusion that objectivity, even if unattainable, is desirable (if it were, it would surely be constitutive value No. 1). Consequently, "...the biggest problem with technology assessment and environmental-impact analysis is not how to make them completely neutral, but how to protect ourselves from those who want us to believe that they can be" [Ibid., 99].

Precisely because science is a human undertake, we must not ignore the will to know which shapes it. A fortiori the same is true in ethics, aesthetics and politics. Hence, for Nozick (just as for C.I.Lewis and Ralph Barton Perry), we must beware of false abstractions. Values mean nothing apart from valuers; norms are constructs which cannot be understood except in embodied relation to those who create, share and sustain them. Reified value is a paradigm case of misplaced concreteness. This leads Nozick to espouse a mild form of voluntarism, which he calls "realizationism". Realizationism holds that "we choose or determine that there be values, that they exist, but their character is independent of us" [Nozick (1981), 555]. The "independence" is reminiscent of the 'third world' of abstractions posited in Karl Popper's ontology [Ibid., 556]. Nozick concludes that the f/v dichotomy is not bogus, but merely in need of qualification: "Particular facts F do not entail particular value or ought statements. V. An additional premise is needed, namely: there is value...The gap between fact and value, [is] bridged but not erased by our reflexive choice that there be value...." [Ibid., 567, 570; parenthetical added]. Christine Korsgaard reaffirms this idea in her own way, at the conclusion of her penetrating paper on goodness in Moore and Kant: "If human beings have an intrinsic value by virtue of the capacity for valuing things, then human beings bring goodness into the world" [Korsgaard (1983), 195]. This is exactly the guideline Nozick adopts.

Or perhaps it is a sign of the times. The Owl of Minerva flies during periods of darkness. After Vietnam and Watergate, our country remains imperiled and in need of intellectual leadership. Some day, historians may not find it surprising that as confidence in our civilization declined, interest in "applied" and normative value questions rose and resurfaced as never before. Monocausal explanations are invariably simplistic. Influence of such diverse factors as the Supreme Court's 1973 and 1986 abortion rulings, the controversies surrounding recombinant DNA, and the computer revolution must all be assessed in accounting for the changes in American philosophers' professional allegiances. Nor should we overlook the contributions of individuals, such as

John Rawls, whose magisterial work in political theory set an example for combining professionalism and rigor with classical scope and depth. Whatever the causes, Nozick's pronouncements do reflect the spirit of the age. They are no less courageous for that, although Nozick does strike a final compromise with conventional f/v wisdom.

Does this compromise need to be made? Suppose we give Nozick's ontological speculations the benefit of the doubt, just for argument's sake. Then it might be reasonable to ask the following: (a) If we choose to bring value into the world, is such choice a fact, the outcome of a (logically) prior value assessment, or both? Or, (b) is there a third category which transcends and synthesizes fact and value? Moreover, (c) is value created directly, or only by choosing to create a "meta-value" (e.g., the value of realizationism) as its logical ancestor? Nozick tries to avoid the prospect of an infinite regress by appealing to mystical experience and "organic unity," but these are of no avail. The problem with Nozick's approach is that he does not remain faithful to his original approach, which challenged the f/v dichotomy by subverting the alleged neutrality of fact. This was all that was necessary to undermine the orthodox view from within. Further ploys were superfluous, and could only succeed in fudging the original argument.

If we turn to Lewis, we can appreciate why this happened to Nozick, and how it might be avoided. Let us begin by delineating the ideas that they have in common. Writing shortly after World War II, Lewis most strenuously insists that "the denial to value-apprehensions in general of the character of truth or falsity and of knowledge, would imply both moral and practical cynicism...if action in general is pointless, then knowledge is also futile, and one belief is as good as another" [Lewis (1946), 366]. I interpret this as synonymous with Nozick's initial point about the interpenetration between fact and value. If nothing has value, then facts cannot have any value, either. Shifting to the linguistic realm, if value-propositions are meaningless, then what are we to say about 'x is a fact,' for any x? Can we say that it is true (or false), without committing ourselves to a thesis about normative significance which has just been outlawed? Nozick is right--values enter into the very definition of what a fact is. This is why Lewis reminds us that "Those who...tell us that there are no valid norms or binding imperatives, are hopelessly confused, and inconsistent with their own...assertion." [Ibid., 480-481]. Consequently, "there is one principle no self-governing creature can adopt--the principle of having no principles. There is one imperative he cannot heed--the imperative to heed no imperatives; one resolution he cannot follow--the resolution to disregard all resolutions" [Lewis (1969), 73]. The "practical contradictions" [Ibid., 67] which flow from acceptance of a f/v dichotomy are both paralyzing and a cogent proof of its mistakenness. Nor is reduction to absurdity purchased at the expense of attacking a straw arguer. For if we sharply "distinguish" fact from value, yet without drawing extreme consequences, then what is left of the distinction except a harmless verbalism, like Dewey's potato/value disjunction? Suppose that inductive, as opposed to deductive, reasoning were able to bridge the gap between fact and value. Would philosophers accept this, yet continue to stress the presence of a "gap" of some kind? I, like Hampshire, doubt it, for the distinction would serve no purpose were it not in the service of a derogatory thesis about value. That such denigration is itself the expression of a (misguided) valuation is the final self-mockery attending the whole subject. Lewis hammers at such points, whereas Nozick merely flirts with them; yet there is undeniable kinship between their respective views (and with the position maintained here).

Despite Lewis' achievement in routing the f/v ideology, even he concedes that in one respect the reductio falls short of its goal. No moral axiom or imperative can be fully self-justifying, or "rest upon logical argument" entirely. Why does Lewis hesitate? Because all arguments presume the existence of a rational agent, one who "...will respond to considerations of consistency and inconsistency," rather than "...be impervious to any concern for the future" or for anything beyond "momentary attitudes." A being with whom we cannot communicate, who resists all appeals to reason, resembles nothing so much as a "fish or a phonograph-record," conversation with whom would be pointless [Lewis (1946), 481].

This passage invites several glosses.

(i) My first reaction is to say, so what? Algebra and geometry aren't self-justifying either, for the same reason. The pervasive features of human (or rational) communication do not plague value-theory any more than they may haunt arithmetic. (This issue will resurface when we study Moore closely.)

(ii) Lewis' overriding motives make these remarks understandable. He wished to harmonize a priori method (based on Kant) with testable propositions about human good (based on pragmatism and, to a lesser extent, the utilitarian tradition). Seeing imperatives as grounded in "a datum of human nature" enabled him to have it both ways. Or so he thought. Whether Lewis' project is viable or not, we can grasp why it was natural for him to say such things. Further discussion of Lewis would constitute a digression. However, momentarily we shall provide a vindication of his general methodology, if not of his specific proposals.

(iii) The inferences which Lewis upholds are by no means bizarre or obsolete. Consider the case of Alan Gewirth. Gewirth defends what he calls the "principle of generic consistency" ("act in accord with the generic rights of your recipients as well as yourself" [Gewirth (1978), 135]). He refers to PGC as a "substantial necessary truth that sets overriding requirements for all agents" [Ibid., 365], describes it as being "categorical and objectively valid" [Ibid., 161], and calls it "the supreme principle of the whole field of action because of its derivation from the generic features and normative structure of action" [Ibid., 148]--a significant linking up of metaphysical and moral claims. Moreover, "it is impossible to refrain from committing oneself to...the generic features of action, for any such refraining would itself exhibit those features" [Ibid., 357]. Sounds like Lewis, doesn't it? Nor does the resemblance end there; for Gewirth also maintains that "the PGC is formally or logically necessary in that any agent who denies or refuses to accept it contradicts himself" [Ibid., 150]. And, again like Lewis, Gewirth recognizes that his own derivation of 'ought' from 'is' [Ibid., 149, 159] is limited by one condition: "...the value-judgments and right-claims it elicits from within the standpoint of the agent are...accepted ...on pain of

irrationality" [Ibid., 161]. If an agent does not
wish to be rational, then (s)he and Gewirth must part
company. Although Gewirth does his best to defend a
"modified naturalism" which includes reference to
"what agents logically must admit or accept" [Ibid.,
363], even he admits that "...prescriptiveness
stems ultimately from the conativeness of purposive
action" [Ibidem]. In other words, if I want to be
rational I must play by Gewirth's rules. But
nothing logically compels me to desire rationality. We may freely grant that X "...must be
desired or valued by all persons insofar as they are
rational agents" [Ibid., 161]. But what about
insofar as they are not, and do not wish to be,
rational agents? Because Gewirth is less frank about
the limits of apodicticity than Lewis, the
"dialectically necessary argument" that he elaborates
does not live up to its own advertisement. Lewis, on
the other hand, is more candid than he needs to be,
since (as we explained in (i) above) the shortcoming
in his argument is shared by every discipline, and is
by no means unique to axiology. Yet the similarities
between their respective doctrines are what is
striking, the more so as Gewirth never mentions Lewis
and appears to have arrived at the same conclusions
quite independently.

(iv) I suspect that what troubles Nozick is
closely akin to what disturbs other philosophers.
What Nozick means when he says "we choose or
determine that there be values, that they exist..."
[Nozick (1981), 555] is precisely what Gewirth terms
"conativeness" and Lewis calls a "datum" about the
species. Nozick misleadingly (and exaggeratedly)
resorts to a form of voluntarism to get the idea
across, but that should not deter us from
appreciating (or rectifying) it. The need to
demystify and reinterpret Nozick's text should not
prevent us from acknowledging and following his sound
intuition as far as we can. Perhaps Nozick's only
mistake is to suppose that he has bridged the f/v
gap by introducing the sole postulate "there is
value." That is true, and it expresses a basic fact
about us as creatures. But it is also true that
"there are facts," and this likewise expresses a
basic value about us, namely, the demand for truth.
Without such a coincidence of alleged opposites, the
analysis of f/v must remain incomplete.

Incidentally, what we have just said enjoins no serious modifications of the thesis that facts belong to the domain of values [Chapter I, p. 2]. A truth about values is a fact, and as such presupposes yet another value. Hence, there is no categoreal parity between fact and value; alternatively stated, value always has a higher cardinality than fact, more or less as Robert Hartman supposes [Hartman (1967), 117, 144]. This topic awaits further development, at the end of Chapter VI.

We will look at some European challenges to f/v later on [Chapter X, pp. 120ff]. Meanwhile, we should advance toward <u>Principia Ethica.</u>

CHAPTER IV

THE TEXTBOOK MOORE

According to the presentation of Moore that several generations of thinkers have grown up with, (1) 'good' is indefinable, (2) all attempts to define 'good' commit the naturalistic fallacy, (3) 'good' is a non-natural property which (somehow) attaches itself to natural objects, and (4) propositions about specific cases of goodness are neither logically nor empirically defensible, but are accessible only to (fallible) intuition. Now that we are ready for our qualifying examinations in ethics, we can proceed in one of two ways: quick dismissal of Moore or pain-staking examination of his canonic texts. I choose the latter course, despite whatever irritation it may cause. Moore is a boring writer, and often a poor one. It is not true that he asserts more than argues his case [MacIntyre (1984), 16], yet his arguments are often so sloppy that they hide their major premises. Yet he is someone we cannot ignore. The naturalistic fallacy continues to be influential; it is widely thought to demonstrate the existence of a f/v chasm and therefore to dictate the course that value theory must follow.

As often happens, the actual study of Moore is rewarding in ways far different from what his reputation might lead one to expect. Yet he is also a difficult writer to understand, and teasing out the most plausible interpretation from his often obscure comments is (at best) a difficult and time-consuming chore. Moore is definitely an acquired taste, and it takes perseverance (or else perversity) to enjoy his thought. Yet he has many things of paramount importance to tell us, and even his errors are instructive and memorable. Once he was revered as the father of philosophical analysis; nowadays he suffers from benign neglect, and is written about only by a few specialists. This is a pity. Unfortunately, there is no short-cut method by which to demonstrate that it is worth the effort to probe his works. However, armed with the excuse afforded by the need to review the naturalistic fallacy, perhaps we can coax ourselves into absorbing more of Moore as we go along.

CHAPTER V

A GUIDED TOUR OF PRINCIPIA ETHICA (PE), CHAPTER I

A. The Naturalistic Fallacy (NF)

The historical importance of the fallacy and its systematic connection with issues already scrutinized make it the obvious candidate for immediate study. The important thing to remember about the naturalistic fallacy (NF) is that there is more than one version of it. Failure to realize this can engender all sorts of confusion. Textbook summaries of Moore generally offer one or at most two accounts. This is not due to poor scholarship; Moore himself never showed any awareness that he had produced a plethora of distinct formulations, and hence, always referred to "the" NF as though it were univocal. Perhaps it is; but we cannot comprehend its essence without first unfolding it in its lushest variety. I will make no advance promises about my exegesis. But one comment is in order: treating the NF as a single (underlying) idea works only if the idea is well chosen. The accounts offered in secondary sources are easy to find philosophical fault with; they leave the reader wondering why Moore still commands such respect. I should prefer you to come away from this book believing in the existence of a dozen NFs, some of which have intellectual merit, than to reduce the NF to a single scheme which may be worthless.

My first attempt to expose the plurality of NFs occurred in 1982. The enumeration corresponds to itemized statements in Chapter I of PE. Since this list will be superseded, there is no reason to burden the reader (yet) with extensive textual quotations. But the old summary will be useful for initiating discussion. Accordingly, I reproduce it below [cf. Rohatyn (1982), 173]. Moore claims that the NF occurs whenever we:

(1) construe value propositions as analytic, rather than synthetic [PE 7] (Moore speaks only of ethics, but we will give the widest possible scope to his allegations).

(2) Identify 'good' with any other property [PE 10].

(3) Define 'good,' thereby precluding any debate over its meaning [PE 11].

20

(4) Substitute a statement about how words are used (lexicography) for an analysis of what 'good' really means [PE 11-12].

(5) Confuse two distinct predicates (objects), regardless of whether both are "natural" or one is natural and the other, non-natural [PE 12-13].

Version (5) has been christened the "definist fallacy" [Frankena (1939), repr. in Klemke (1969), 37-38], and has been attacked from many sides. But as we can see, it is just one of the weapons in Moore's arsenal. Resuming the list:

(6) Fail to recognize that two predicates (objects) cannot meaningfully be compared unless they are irreducibly distinct [PE 14-15].

(7) Confuse 'good' with a complex whole [PE 15].

(8) Ignore the infinite regress characterizing all serious moral debate [PE 15-16].

Version (8) is the "open-question" argument, and it requires unpacking in its own right, which we will do later. Meanwhile, continuing the list:

(9) Assume that 'good' is meaningless [PE 16].

(10) Beg the question concerning the adoption of a value-standard; smuggle an assumption into a value-related argument, while pretending that it has already been justified or that it is self-evidently true [PE 18-19].

(11) Offer nothing but fallacious reasons in support of a value-standard [PE 20-21].

(12) Both define and use any given value-term, which results in a begged question concerning the stipulation or what follows from (accepting) it [PE 20-21].

See what I mean about "the" NF? It would be foolish to deny that there are close resemblances between (2) and (5), or among (3), (8), (10) and (12). But I defy anyone to inspect this list and find any easy common denominator for all twelve! And why should (s)he? There is plenty of interesting material to work on, in advance of any synthesis. This was the secret of Moore's genius; a secret he kept from himself. By bombarding the reader with a multitude of "fallacies," all catalogued as one and the same, Moore scored an impressive debater's triumph. The odds that Moore can persuade you of the cogency of his polemic increase with the number of versions of the NF that he propounds. His reasoning appears convergent, even if it isn't. Sooner or later you are bound to find something logically attractive (and/or emotionally resonant) in his systematically ambiguous appeals. Even once the ambiguity is detected, this does not spoil Moore's party. Important philosophical words have always been notorious for their conceptual richness. Moreover, there is no doubt about the absence of sophistical manipulation. Like Thomas Kuhn, who has at least twenty-one different senses of 'paradigm' [Masterman, in Lakatos and Musgrave (1970), 61-65], Moore is unconscious of what he is doing, and would no doubt have been horrified if someone had ever pointed it out to him. We are lucky that he did not catch it himself, in 1903, in spite of the subsequent (temporary!) damage inflicted on value-theory. Most scholars are very familiar with versions 5 and 8, above. Hence, the other ten statements of the NF do not receive as much attention. My conviction is that 8 is the central argument, and that the other eleven are subordinate to it. But this is arguable, nor should it mislead anyone into imagining that all but one of Moore's pronouncements may be discounted.

The above list is faithful to the order in which Moore exposits the NF. As a consequence, it is cumbrous and redundant in places. So let's try a second approach to itemization, streamlining both the number of formulations and their wording. The reader who has gone through points (1)-(12) above will have no difficulty in noting various correspondences between this new synopsis and its precessor.

Second précis: Moore alleges that the NF occurs if and only if we:

(a) assume that value propositions are tautologies or more verbal equivalences [PE 7].

(b) Equate 'good' with anything else [PE 10].

(c) Define 'good' [PE 11].

(d) Assume that 'good' is meaningless [PE 16].

(e) Define a value-term in order to excuse employing it in an antecedently favored way [PE 20-21].

(f) Arbitrarily legislate the correctness of a given value-standard [PE 20-21].

(g) Treat any value axiom as self-evident, or as requiring no further justification [PE 18-19].

(h) Ignore the endless debatability (in principle) of any value-thesis [PE 15-16].

Version (h) is the open-question argument (OQA) once more. But this time, there are prospects for unification of the NF that were not open to us before. This will become clear as soon as we explicate the OQA. Since I do regard the OQA as Moore's most basic argument, it should be quoted at length:

> I. The hypothesis that disagreement about good is disagreement with regard to the correct analysis of a given whole, may be most plainly seen to be incorrect by consideration of the fact that, whatever definition be offered, it may always be asked, with significance, of the complex so defined, whether it is itself good [PE 15].

Moore than gives a famous (and hard to repeat!) example:

> II. To take, for instance, one of the more plausible, because one of the more complicated, of such proposed definitions, it may easily be thought, at first sight, that to be good may mean to be that which we desire to desire [PE 15].

However, this proves incorrect, and needlessly convoluted:

> III....if we carry the investigation further, and ask ourselves 'is it good to desire to desire A?' it is apparent, on a little reflection, that this question is itself as intelligible, as the original question 'Is A good?'--that we are, in fact, now asking for exactly the same information about the desire to desire A,

23

for which we formerly asked with regard to
A itself [PE 15-16].

The moral is then drawn:

> IV....it is also apparent that the
> meaning of this second question cannot be
> correctly analyzed into 'Is the desire to
> desire A one of the things which we desire
> to desire?': we have not before our minds
> anything so complicated as the question 'Do
> we desire to desire to desire A?' [PE 16].

Moore goes on to say that we can discern "by inspection" that:

> V....the predicate of this proposition—
> 'good'—is positively different from the
> notion of 'desiring to desire' which enters
> into its subject: 'That we should desire
> to desire A is good' is <u>not</u> merely
> equivalent to 'That A should be good is
> good' [PE, M.s italics].

The conclusions of Moore's analysis call attention to the distinction between intensional and extensional forms of equivalence:

> VI. It may indeed be true that what we
> desire to desire is always also good;
> perhaps, even the converse may be true; but
> it is very doubtful whether this is the
> case, and the mere fact that we understand
> very well what is meant by doubting it,
> shows clearly that we have two different
> notions before our minds [PE 16].

This passage invites extended commentary, ranging from trivial to sublime:

    1. Moore employed single quotes to distinguish between what Carnap would later term mention (<u>vs</u>. use) of an expression. However, he is not consistent in this regard; compare quotation V. with I., II., and III., for example. When he wants to distinguish between meaning and reference, he will introduce the expression "<u>the</u> good" [PE 9], but even this policy is not strictly adhered to.

    2. The term "open-question" is used not here, but (for the first time) at PE 21, in commenting

(retrospectively) on version (12) (or f.) of the NF. Yet commentators have not erred in assigning it to the textually prior (8) (or h.), which is where it rightly belongs. The label does not matter, but it does fit Moore's intent and by now is customary.

3. It is wise to disregard Moore's own penchant for mentalism, as in his many remarks about "holding up" propositions for inner adjudication. This is neither to deny the influence of the phenomenological school (Brentano) on Moore's thought at the turn of the century, nor to disregard his emphasis on intuition, which plays such a major role in Chapters. V and VI of PE. It is merely to say that all such statements can be translated into a linguistic mode if we prefer to consider them that way. Moore's logic is unaffected, and may even be aided, by such maneuvers. Hence, for such locutions as "having two different notions before our minds," we may substitute 'using two non-equivalent terms.'

4. Since the goodness (desirability) of A is not reducible to any concatenation of statements about its being desired, the bearing of the passage (e.g., quote II) on upholding the fact/value dichotomy should be apparent. The test is meant to be perfectly arbitrary, i.e., devoid of any peculiarities that might render its logical lesson inapplicable elsewhere. Moore's example is by no means (pedagogically) simple, but it serves as a basis for warning us about contexts in which the same problem arises. Hence, it is clear that Moore intends for us to generalize from this to all similar cases, although he does not bother to make this explicit. It is premature to criticize Moore's argument insofar as it purports to make the f/v dichotomy conceptually unavoidable. We will have plenty of time to berate him later, if necessary!

5. The claim that one must never confuse desire (fact) with desirability (value or norm) is made again in Chap. III [PE 66,72], in reviewing J.S. Mill's alleged proof of utility. We will not pause to examine Moore's reconstruction of Mill in any detail, but see Rohatyn (1976), Chapter III.

6. The OQA tells us that every set of value-axioms is arbitrary, i.e., contains at least one unprovable proposition as an element. So what else is new? Aristotle already recognized the existence of indemonstrables, requiring (logically) prior acts

of nous as their sole avenue of establishment [Post. An. 72b20, 92b35-39, 100b9 ff; cf. PE 144]. Should anyone lose any sleep over the fact that "equals added to equals give equals" is unprovable, but must be assumed in order to make proofs possible? Granted, there are times when assumptions can be challenged--Euclid's 5th (parallel) postulate is a famous case in point. But the OQA lumps together the genuine with the spurious cases of debatability. Surely there is a difference between innocuous and loaded assumptions, whether in ethics or mathematics. If the latter can live with arbitrariness, and discriminate between cases that are worth further scrutiny and those that aren't, why can't the former be permitted the same privilege? We might think that the answer is that in value-related issues it is difficult to achieve consensus. Granted; but Moore's objection is that consensus is no better than an ad populum appeal, since it is always possible to question its validity. It is also possible to ask "why?" an indefinite number of times, as small children often do; the questions soon become tedious and a mere nuisance, even if the child never tires of asking them. Some (indefinitely repeated) questions have a point, others do not, or else obey a law of diminishing intellectual returns. [On open vs. closed questions, see Rohatyn (1976), 83; Orenduff (1980), 160; and Stout (1981), 197-198.]

So let us concede to Moore that he has anticipated Goedel (by 28 years) in discovering the value analogue of undecidability in first-order predicate logic. What difference does it make, and why should we honor Moore rather than his 17th-19th century predecessors [Prior (1949), 106-107], who lay posthumous claim to the same accomplishment?

The answer lies in what (since Kant) we have come to know as the 'binding power of the norm.' Unlike Aristotle, who was content with the limitations of "practical science," we demand absolute correctness from value assertions, perhaps because contemporary life is so complicated that we yearn for simple solutions. We have learned to accept uncertainty in physics, and incompleteness in mathematics. However, too much is at stake in a nuclear era for us to be at ease with tentative and defeasible hypotheses in ethics; this concedes too much ground to the enemy, i.e., relativism. Moore's proof that value questions are open succeeds in direct proposition to our half-conscious desire to close them, once and for all. The anxiety we experience when we realize that such closure is impossible in principle, only increases our sense of intellectual tension, and makes us want this all the more. This feeling unwittingly plays into Moore's hands. Trotsky once said that persons desiring a quiet life have made a mistake by being born in the 20th century. The dilemmas of contemporary life create a crisis mentality, as innumerable authors (Ellul, Erikson, Fromm, Mumford) have shown. The OQA thrives on fear.

As a product of the Edwardian age, Moore was sensitive to the need for stability. Yet his logical acumen and scrupulosity combine [in Chapter I of PE] to put complacency to rout. Has the bottom dropped out? Not for Moore, even if his successors sometimes oscillated between existential despair and "commitment" on one hand, and the shallowness of emotivism on the other. Why is Moore so calm in the midst of his own storm? Version 9. (or d.) supplies the clue. After finishing the OQA, Moore goes on to remark that:

>VII....the same consideration is sufficient to dismiss the hypothesis that 'good' has no meaning whatsoever [PE 16].

Moore then reminds us of the difference between tautologies ("identical propositions") and mere generalizations ("universal ethical principles"). He reiterates, this time with a different example, that:

>VIII....whoever will attentively consider with himself what is actually before his mind when he asks the question 'is pleasure (or whatever it may be) after all good?' can easily satisfy himself that he is not merely wondering whether pleasure is pleasant [PE 16].

By performing a "succession" of such thought "experiments," one:

>IX....may become expert enough to recognize that in every case he has before his mind a unique object, with regard to the connection of which with any other object, a distinct question may be asked. Everyone does in fact understand the question 'Is this good?'...[PE 16-17].

Critics have (rightly) harped on the fact that Moore is here introducing his own conception of 'good' as the name of a non-natural object. What is a non-natural object, and are there any such things? Besides, even if Moore can answer both of these questions, what bearing does this have on the NF? Must we accept Moore's own constructive account of what 'good' is in order to accuse alternative accounts of being defective? If so, then perhaps it is Moore rather than his rivals who is guilty of begging the question in his own favor.

For precisely these reasons, it is best to follow the strategy recommended in 3. on p. 25. For "unique object" substitute "different term/symbol/concept," and the passage becomes quite harmless. Moore himself licenses such an approach when he says, a moment later, that 'good' "...has a distinct meaning" for any thinker, even though (s)he "...may not recognize in what respect it is distinct" [PE 17]. For all his vaunted carefulness with words, Moore was very lax about the difference between "notions" and the "states of mind" which may or may not accompany them. The historical reasons for this fuzziness are not hard to trace, although they lie outside our purview. What Moore was careful to say is that the explicit awareness of the difference between 'good' and other notions is required "for correct ethical reasoning" [PE 17], presumably in philosophy though not in everyday life. Hence, the universal understanding of 'is this good?' is not something immediate, but might disclose itself under the pressure of Socratic or cross-examination.

When freed of mentalism, the passage above avoids being hoisted with Moore's own naturalistic petard. More importantly, it shows us why Moore did not regard the NF as the portent of disaster for value-theory that later writers were forced to confront. 'Good' <u>must</u> be meaningful, for the same reason that makes ethical debate never-ending. If we didn't understand what 'good' meant, we couldn't even begin to argue about it, or to disagree, whether intelligently or unintelligently. The fact that we can argue and communicate our differences is a permanently hopeful sign, even amidst the ruins of logically interminable back-and-forth. The condition for defending indefinitely prolonged discourse is that it never degenerate. Just as Moore did not realize how many NFs there were, so too it never occurred to him that his critique of classical systems might be taken as a signal to abandon their subject. In both cases, Moore has suffered from misinterpretation, or else, like other giants, has had his original purpose diverted to serve other causes. The recovery of Moore's intent yields an unexpected bonus for value-theory, provided we have the patience to carry out the salvage operation.

7. Since the reasoning behind the OQA (versions (8), h.) is used to repudiate (9) or d., an hypothesis suggests itself: Why not extend this technique to the remaining versions, to see whether they can be comprehended in similar fashion? Let's begin this task by looking at the claim that value (ethical) propositions are always synthetic, never analytic. This just doesn't seem right. For one thing, it makes value-theory into an empirical discipline, utilizing the very naturalism that Moore supposedly attacks. Also, if 'good' is indefinable, how can it become part of a body of synthetic propositions? Last, if 'good' names a non-natural property or object [PE 41], doesn't this rule syntheticity out altogether? Not a promising start. Jager (1969) has documented the early Moore's fondness for Kantian terminology, but if the NF is to be credible, it must adopt such vocabulary without destroying itself.

Here is where the OQA comes to the rescue. Moore's reasoning is as follows: If ethical propositions were analytic, they would be (in effect) definitions, hence not debatable. But that would make ethical controversy pointless, and ethical propositions trivial and uninformative. Moreover, it would result in complete arbitrariness. I legislate my point of view, you legislate yours, hence we can each appeal (in wholly circular fashion) only to our own initial posits to "justify" our ideas and exclude those of our opponents. The upshot is that dialogue gives way to an unprofitable sequence of monologues, and competing ideologies become (as Popper might say) closed rather than open. The only alternative, therefore, is to label value statements as synthetic. This does not mean that they can be (dis)confirmed by experience; hence Moore's choice of terms is misleading and inappropriate. But we can at least grasp what led him to make such a startling pronouncement. Not only does this enable us to derive version (1) (or a.) from the OQA, but it does exactly the same for versions (10) and (12) on the first list, and for e., f., and g. on the second list. The NF begins to look like a theme with multiple variations, rather than a cacophonous collection of unrelated melodies.

We can carry this process of unification one step further. The heart of the OQA is the contention that it is always possible (intelligible) to doubt any alleged equation involving 'good.' We might compare Moore to Descartes (rather than Goedel) as having made value-skepticism into a methodical principle. (I will bypass any problems this may raise in connection with Moore's defense of common sense or his proof of an external world.) If we accept such doubt as legitimate and (in theory) well-founded, then it follows that we are committed to denying the possibility of defining 'good,' whether in lexical (version (4)) or any other terms. Hence, we get versions (2), (3), (5), and (6); likewise, b. and c. fall into place. Quotations I. and VI. show, too, why Moore adopted Bishop Butler's maxim ("everything is what it is, and not another thing") as the motto of his book. Perhaps he should have quoted Parmenides' fragment 5, 'It is all the same to me where I begin, for there I shall return,' as well. We began by expanding the number of NFs, from one to twelve (or eight). We have now contracted it down to one again, not out of a penchant for monistic explanation but because the data do fit the hypothesis.

8. To summarize: definitions of 'good' (or any other value-term) beg the question, because the adoption of any standard runs into the infinite regress problem. Any attempt to circumvent this is nothing but an arbitrary stipulation--a verbal solution to an intellectual problem. If two (or $\underline{n}$) predicates were not distinct from one another, they could not meaningfully be compared. Even if all X is Y, the 'is' of predication must never be confused with the 'is' of identity. Even if all X is Y and all Y is X, the extensional equivalence between X and Y does not warrant any claims to intentional equivalence, synonymy, identity, or the production of pseudo-tautologies based on such claims. Moore repeats this message in 1942 [PGEM, 599, 610; also see Fogelin (1967), 124, and Broad (1970), 366]. The invalidity of such inferences is a simple matter of logic, not something suspiciously devised or framed <u>ad hoc</u>. Hence the potency of Moore's admonition against committing fallacies-- propounding arguments which seem sound, yet aren't

[Hamblin (1970), 12]. The fallacy is the same, no matter when and where it is committed; it is "called naturalistic with reference to Ethics ...its being made with regard to 'good' marks it as something quite specific, and this specific mistake deserves a name because it is so common" [PE 13].

Thanks to the OQA, 'good' is indefinable. If it were the other way around--if the OQA were justified in light of the indefinability of 'good'--then Moore would indeed be begging the question on his own behalf. Not only is the indefinability of 'good' "...logically independent of the proposition that goodness is non-natural" [Frankena (1939), repr. in Klemke (1969), 39], but the entire discussion of indefinability needs to be grounded in the defense of the OQA, lest Moore's entire house of fallacies crumble. To reconstruct the text in the strongest possible terms requires making the OQA the dominant, indeed the sole argument; all the remaining versions are corollaries, radiating outward from the center of PE Chap. I. Moore's innocence in regarding the NF as a univocal concept is pardonable after all, despite his carelessness.

9. Several problems still face us. In 1922, Moore wrote a preface for the revised edition of PE. However, it was not published then, or even during Moore's lifetime. We have only been able to glimpse its contents since 1964. In it, he rueshaving given the impression that the indefinability of 'good' was a mere deduction from the sweeping indefinability of words in general (the exact accusation that Frankena was to make in 1939, 17 years later), and regrets failing to distinguish between definability on one hand, and analyzability on the other. He then reinterprets the NF as (1) the equation between Good and a natural (or metaphysical) property, or (ii) inferences stemming from such an equation [Lewy (1964), repr. in Ambrose and Lazerowitz (1970), 296-297]. It is a pity that Moore chose not to publish the preface; doing so might have avoided many subsequent misunderstandings. Yet, the preface does not make it substantially easier to ferret out the true meaning of the NF, because we still demand a reason why the equation between 'good' and any other property is forbidden. Couldn't we challenge Moore on precisely the OQAish grounds that he adopts in Chapter I? Hence we are not put at ease by Moore's assurance that indefinability is not a major issue. If it's not, what is? Looked at another way, even if

we give up all the versions of the NF in which indefinability plays a role, we are still left with (1), (4), (7)-(12) from the first list, or a., and d.-h. from the second list. So the burden, first of unfolding the variety of NFs and then of unifying them, has not been significantly lightened. It is nice to know that the indefinability of 'good' is subordinate to some other considerations; this reinforces our conclusion that indefinability must follow from more basic lines of argument. But Moore gives us no clue as to what these might be; like many original thinkers, he is not the most reliable guide to his own work. Whatever doubts Moore's preface might have assuaged, it was not capable of unravelling the textual knots which he tied so expertly in PE.

As long as we are discussing indefinability, I must state bluntly that I do not find anything Moore said on that topic after 1903 terribly illuminating. In 1932, looking back on PE, he disarmingly confessed that "...all the supposed proofs were certainly fallacious" [repr. in Moore (1959), 98]. Yet he does not retract the claim that "very likely" 'good' really is indefinable, and that no good arguments have been brought forward to show that it isn't! Something may of course be the case even if it cannot (yet) be proved, yet Moore's hairline consistency is more annoying than candid. This remark was made ten years after the unpublished reflection on PE; and it is no more helpful. Another ten years went by before Moore returned to the subject a final time in 1942, where his brief remarks suggest that 'good' is not merely indefinable as a certain genus, but indefinable <u>simpliciter</u> [PGEM 594-595]. These are not the thoughts of someone who regretted the boldness of his youthful position. Indeed, his last published verdict is that neither 'good' nor 'ought' is definable--let alone, one in terms of the other [PGEM 610]. Perhaps Moore's suppression of his 1922 literary Nachlass is not such a tragedy.

10. I have deliberately refrained from saying anything yet about the concept of intrinsic value. This is a separate and fascinating topic which will get its due share of attention later. It is important to distinguish, at least provisionally, Moore's constructive attempts to do normative ethics and aesthetics from his major (destructive) critique of the traditions and systems that precede him. Eventually we will be in a position to bring these

two topics together, but only after the exposition has been developed in an orderly sequence. We will find that while Moore always remained overtly faithful to the f/v dichotomy [see PGEM 568], he was a closet subversive who never became explicitly aware of his own rebellion against the doctrine he helped to found. So, when Moore admits that the major premises of PE were simultaneously normative and non-normative [PGEM 569], it never occurs to him that he might be compromising the purity of a f/v segregation by making such a concession. As mentioned a moment ago, he is not a keen self-observer. For this reason, I prefer to concentrate on the unspoiled, if tangled, insights of 1903 (and sometimes, 1912), looking at later pieces of self-reflection only occasionally and whenever necessary.

The book that made Moore internationally famous, that permanently established his reputation, had both an official and an unofficial side to it. The "reluctant naturalist" belongs, as we shall see, to the side that Moore always kept disguised--ultimately, from himself.

11. When we contemplate the number of authors who have grown timid under the gaze of the NF (and the OQA, in particular), we realize that it is impossible to overrate its impact on our culture. Even those who defend "cognitive teleology" [Rescher (1977), 18] suddenly find that they cannot transfer "the primacy of praxis" from science to ethics. It never occurs to them that there might be something value-laden in science itself, or that this might enable them to bring off the transition. Instead, we learn that "...the deepest thinkers...have always insisted that there is and can be no...connection" [Ibid., 290, R.s italics) between the "cognitive realm" and the "normative" domain. Once again, fact/value dichotomies cast a shadow over "principles of legitimation" [Ibid., 294), so that dualism awaits its Aufhebung. Rescher does not say who these deep thinkers are--Hume? Kant? G.E. Moore? But when (e.g.) a pragmatist flees from his own system, something must scare him quite badly. Whatever continues to inhibit and to exert such a hold on the ablest and most talented minds must be dealt with as an enemy, and, like all enemies, must not be underestimated. The NF falls into this category. Yet, Moore is no villain, and there are certain respects in which he even qualifies as a hero. We shall soon determine just what these virtuous and redeeming qualities were

B. The Principle of Organic Unities (POU)

Two questions are worth asking here: (1) What is the POU? and (2) Why does Moore bother to introduce it [PE 27-31]?

The first question can be answered straightforwardly, though I will depart from Moore's own wordy rationale in giving its gist. The POU maintains that "the value of...a whole bears no regular proportion to the sum of the values of its parts" [PE 27, orig. in ital.]. Neglect of this principle leads to serious mistakes. The existence of a whole *is* dependent on the concatenation of its parts. Hence, it is plausible (though mistaken) to infer that the value of wholes is likewise a function of their constituents. That value does not vary in this way, may be seen by examining some counter-examples. The enigmatic smile of the Mona Lisa "makes" the painting. Neither the smile by itself nor the rest of the canvas without the smile would be very valuable. We cannot simply add and subtract values, the way we do with lengths and widths. Values are gestalts or wholes; they cannot be segmented or moved around like furniture--such rearrangements leave the law of conservation of energy intact, but they have a profound effect on the value of the (new) objects they create. (Here is where the influence of early phenomenologists on Moore may be traceable, although it requires nothing fancier than to acknowledge the difference between quantity and quality.) It is important not to overdo in the other direction. While value is always contextual, it does not follow that we cannot understand any object except as a part of something else, or solely in relation to a (specified) whole. This is the error of Absolute Idealism, which falsely infers that entities, events and processes can only be grasped by integrating them in an all-inclusive metaphysics. If this were the case, then only God or a similarly omniscient being could apprehend particular propositions about (e.g.) thunderstormes, or even the law of gravity, which finite human beings are able to grasp without benefit of an overarching, systematic view of the whole of existence. The coherence theory of knowledge fastens on a valid principle, but then stretches and exaggerates it unbearably, until it breaks down. Besides, the very meaning of 'part' and 'whole,' respectively, suggests that there are differences between parts and wholes which can and must be as fully appreciated as any resemblances. Any philosophy of Oneness is doomed in advance, since it is bound to deny distinctions and, therefore, must take refuge in mysticism or (what is the same) silence. Whatever cannot respect plurality cannot respect itself, since wholes embed themselves in larger wholes, while philosophies are a part of civilization, but not its sum.

Why does Moore discuss this? Actually, he has several reasons.

(i) He is making a strenuous effort to disentangle himself from the Hegelian teachings of his Cambridge mentors (as the coeval publication of "The Refutation of Idealism" in 1903 might likewise indicate, were it not largely directed against Berkeley rather than versus Hegel). Perhaps he even wants to retain a modified form of Idealist metaphysics, purged of what he regards as its worst deficiencies. In any case, some compromise with the position of his college tutors and with the Tennysonian climate of late 19th century British thought is imminent, as Moore's inventory of various phrases used to describe the POU may suggest [PE 30].

(ii) He is setting up his Chapter VI discussion of the "method of absolute isolation" [PE 188] as the test whereby value claims are upheld and ratified. This not only will require him to reintroduce the POU [PE 189-190, 202], but it also depends upon the acknowledgement that it is indeed possible to examine parts apart from wholes--and wholes apart from other wholes. The classical empiricist emphasis on atomicity and discreteness is still found in Moore, complemented by the emphasis on holism that in turn marks Moore (in his best moments) as a synoptic thinker.

(iii) Preparation for Chapter VI is again animated by the motto adopted from Bishop Butler. Wholes are wholes, parts are parts, things are things; comparison is always possible, but presupposes distinguishability. In some ways, PE is a meditation on the theme of identity and difference, as Plato refined it in the <u>Sophist</u>.

(iv) To justify (iii), Moore makes tacit use of the OQA: "...no part contains analytically the whole to which it belongs, or any other parts of that whole. The relation of part to whole is <u>not</u> the same as that of whole to part; and the very definition of the latter is that it does contain analytically that which is said to be its part" [PE 33-34, M.s italics]. If 'whole' and 'part' were synonymous, then there would be no point in having two different words. Moreover, the asymmetry between part and whole would disappear, which is logically absurd (a "self-contradictory doctrine," PE 34). This is exactly similar to Moore's admonition that we can always discriminate between two different notions, just by employing them side-by-side [quote VI., p. 24]. Recall "is pleasure good?" This is not the same as asking 'is everything that is pleasant (also) good,' or vice versa. Moreover, if pleasure = good, then the question would become "is good good?" (or "is pleasure pleasure?") which is trivial (an analyticity), and not the sense intended by the question. The non-substitutability of one value-term for another is established by "holding up" both or all of them for mutual comparison. Here, Moore generalizes this procedure, to make a mockery of purported part-whole equations. This is additional evidence for the superordinate role played by the OQA in PE Chap. I.

(v) Most crucially, here Moore sharply distinguishes between fact and value. The POU, which is interestingly referred to as a "paradox" [PE 27] is relevant to judgments of worth, but largely inapplicable to physical (or metaphysical) problems. Value is always determined independently of anything else [Rohatyn (1982), 185]. Absolute Idealism, like naturalism, tried to join what must be put asunder. The best proof of the futility of trying to connect value with fact is that one and the same object may have a certain value, W, in one context and a very different value, Z, in another. This is a commonplace occurrence, yet it defeats any attempts to make value dependent on (or proportional to) factual status. Not only can we successfully counter-example the thesis that value is based on fact, but (taken to extremes) this reduces itself to absurdity. Hegel and "the whole of orthodox philosophy" [PE 34] at the turn of the century have "...encouraged the self-contradictory belief that one and the same thing may be two different things, and that only in one of its formsis it truly what it is" [PE 35]. The OQA enables us to penetrate this linguistic fog. As Moore's chief dialectical instrument it justifies his emphasis on putting words and entities in their proper places. Thus, the many themes canvassed in PE Chap. I are not a scattered and diverse group, but welded together by relentless, single-minded logic. In this fashion, the opening gambits of PE acquire an impressive organic unity of their own.

The POU is Moore's richest innovation. It synthesizes competing world-views while adding novel insights of its own. It is an undeniably brilliant and skillful ending to a chapter already celebrated as a *tour de force*. What can Moore do for an encore? And does he need one? The reader may be anxious to know whether the POU really establishes an irrevocable f/v distinction, or if it is flawed in some subtle way. I cannot deal with this question until we have seen just how Moore develops and employs the POU, in PE Chap. VI. Like any climax, this should be progressed toward as slowly and tantalizingly as possible, consistent with maintaining hope, interest and enthusiasm. We already know one thing. It is mistaken to believe that "the value of X is the sum of its degree of organic unity plus the values of each of its parts" [Nozick (1981), 423], precisely because "degrees" of unity cannot be measured, while values cannot be summed. Besides, "...organic unity constitutes value only on the assumption that there is value" [*Ibid.*, 567]. No value, no conceivable organic unity.

Ontology beckons.

CHAPTER VI.

INTERMEZZO: ONTOLOGY AND VALUE

If Moore is serious about calling 'good' non-natural, he had best explain what he means. He does this in Chapter II. First, he explains that 'nature' comprises "the subject-matter of the sciences and also of psychology" [PE 40]. He contends, a trifle optimistically, that the existence of (past, present or future) thoughts poses no problem: "It is easy to say which of them are natural, and which (if any) are not natural" [PE 41]. Apparently, Moore's segregation criterion is based on time. Present thoughts are real, and so too are the present effects of past ones. Future thoughts are predictions (probabilistic estimates) about what is not yet real. Moore then switches to the more general dilemma of determining "which among the properties of natural objects are natural properties and which are not" [PE 41]. This leads straightaway to the following:

> X....I do not deny that good is a property of certain natural objects; certain of them, I think, <u>are</u> good; and yet I have said that 'good' itself is not a natural property...my test for these too also concerns their existence in time [PE 41; M.s italics].

Moore proceeds to give us his criterion for deciding this issue:

> XI. Can we imagine 'good' as existing <u>by itself</u> in time, and not merely as a property of some natural object?...I cannot so imagine it, whereas with the greater number of properties of objects--those which I call the natural properties--their existence does seem to me to be independent of the existence of those objects [PE 41, M.s italics].

Moore then adds that if all the parts of a natural object were removed, "no object would be left, not even a bare substance." By contrast, "...this is not so with good" [PE 41]. (I assume that Moore inadvertently left the single-quotes off.) 'Good' is something over and above a "mere predicate," yet despite its irreducibility, it cannot exist apart from objects. It is nothing without them, even though, (1) it is not a constituent of them, and (2) they are nothing apart from their constituents!

So, what are we left with? According to Moore, 'Good' refers to a non-natural property of natural objects. We can all repeat this strange formula, but does it mean anything? To understand what Moore is up to, we might try on a series of analogies: I. Recall the dispute between Plato and Aristotle over the "separability" of forms. What is the 'form' of a horse, a triangle or of justice? Both Plato and Aristotle agreed that one could not reduce the form to its instances—horses, triangles, just acts. They rejected nominalism, and so (when it comes to 'good') does Moore. But Aristotle held that forms "inhere in" matter. While we can speak of forms, they do not exist apart from objects. Hence, separability is purely a linguistic affair, not the sign of the existence of a special realm of abstract objects. Perhaps all that Moore means by calling 'good' non-natural is that it is logically distinguishable from the objects which exemplify it. This suggestion has been pressed by Hochberg [(1962), repr. in Klemke (1969), 114, 122]. It is advantageous in that it does not prevent Moore from being a Platonist in other respects. "Two *is* somehow, although it does not exist," and "No truth does, in fact, *exist*" [PE 111, M.s italics]. Something can be abstractly real, yet not exist (e.g., as a natural object). Every (wo)man is either a Platonist or an Aristotelian, but there is nothing forbidden or inconsistent about being both, in different contexts.

II. Hochberg's point can be reformulated using Kantian language. Moore tells us that 'good' cannot exist by itself in time. This, rather than existence (or reality) outside time, is what is meant by calling it "non-natural." Hence, the function of the term 'non-natural' is entirely negative and propadeutic. This is reminiscent of Kant's more stringent account of noumena or "things in themselves." These are not hidden entities but thought-standpoints, ways of accounting for the boundaries of (our knowledge of) phenomena, of events in space and time. So long as we avoid reifying these technical terms, we cannot err in ascribing certain meanings to them. Whether Moore was more inclined to (or else familiar with) one way of putting it rather than another makes little difference, and is a minor scruple of historical scholarship.

III. Yet a third parallel is with Hare's notion of supervenience. Although Moore has left Chapter I behind, the NF is still on his mind. For he follows up his comment about the difference between 'good' and "natural properties" by noting that:

> XII. If indeed good were a feeling...then it would exist in time. But that is why to call it so is to commit the naturalistic fallacy. It will always remain pertinent to ask, whether the feeling itself is good; and if so, then good cannot itself be identical with any feeling [PE 41].

(Again, let's forgive Moore's lapse in not supplying single-quotes.) Now why does Moore say this? Note just how tricky his logic is. 'Good' does not exist in time. Do not infer that therefore it exists outside time. 'Good' does not "exist" at all, although there are objects (correctly) described as good. 'Good' is a concept; qua concept it cannot be identified with any state, event, thing or process. This conceptual (as opposed to ontological) independence is what marks 'good' as an intangible, as not denoting part of the universe, exclusive of concepts themselves [cf. Chapter II, pp. 8-9). Hence, no judgment about the world (facts) can possibly shed light on, let alone logically entail, a judgment about 'good' (value), or vice versa; the two categories are utterly discrete. And this is exactly the meaning of supervenience. It is a form of dualism as severe as the Cartesian split between mind and body, the Platonic rift between forms and temporal objects, or the world-view of orthodox Christianity. (Whether all the dualisms can be successfully attacked or refuted in the same manner, as Dewey believed, is another story.)

The paradox involved in taking this third position is obvious. If values neither compel nor are compelled by facts, and if there is (to anticipate Stuart Hampshire) no strongly or weakly inductive relationship between them, either, then how can one ever make (rational) value judgments at all? How do they pass beyond being arbitrary impositions upon data? This was the cardinal dilemma which PE set for several generations of subsequent philosophers, despite Moore's cheerful conclusion that 'good' must be meaningful. Even if we accept that 'good'names a non-natural property of a natural object, we are at a loss to say how (or by what criterion) it does so, in given cases. The analogy with supervenience, though different from either of the first two gambits, fits Moore's intentions equally well, and (in the bargain) entails an apparently doleful outcome both for Hare and himself.

Moore meditated on this problem until the end of his life. In 1942, for example, he commented that an "immense number" of "different natural intrinsic properties" are "ought-implying" [Moore explicates the term 'intrinsic property' at PGEM 584, 605]. But what, as Socrates might ask, do they have in common? Here Moore gropes:

> XIII...there does not seem to be any natural intrinsic property, other than (possibly) the disjunction of them all, which is <u>both</u> entailed by them all and also ought-<u>implying</u> [PGEM 605, M.s italics and parentheses).

This is not a retreat toward nominalism, for in 1903 Moore had said as much about "substances" and their parts, in repudiating the Lockean conception that something remains when the properties of an object are taken away. Thus, Moore continues to insist that "...intrinsic value cannot be identical with <u>any</u> natural intrinsic property" even though "it is entailed by each of them" [PGEM 605-606, M.s italics]. This does for "intrinsic value" what Moore previously did for 'good': elevates it to the status of an Aristotelian form. But (a) If (to appropriate Moore's vocabulary) the set of natural intrinsic properties (p-1 v p-2 v p-3 v...p-n) is ought-implying, doesn't this violate the ban on deriving a value (proposition) from a fact(ual one)? (b) If not, or if for some reason the f/v dichotomy is not affected by this, then (to reiterate the earlier concern) how does one determine just what intrinsic value is, and what (if anything) has got it? Or, has Moore answered this question legalistically, by discriminating between entailment and identity? If so, then his Aristotelianism is harmless, and betrays an underlying naturalism in ethics—just the reverse of what Moore (and his successors) imagined he was doing.

Some 30 years earlier, in 1912, Moore had already staked out the position that determining the class-membership of goodness was impossible:

"...though all these things may...have some characteristic in common, their variety is so great that they have none, which, besides being common to them all, is also peculiar to them...which never belongs to anything which is intrinsically bad or indifferent" [E, 106; M.s italics). This would make Occam's ghost smile. Yet, Moore does offer some criteria for ascertaining 'good,' which amount to necessary (though not sufficient) conditions for its presence: feelings (and forms of consciousness generally), and participation in certain "complex wholes" (E, 103-105, 107]. If the non-naturalness of 'good' meant it was unanalyzable, then even partially spelling out its conditions would be tantamount to committing another fallacy. If the unpublished preface to the second edition of PE is trustworthy, we can see why Moore regretted placing an undue and misleading stress on indefinability, as though silence were the only defensible alternative.

A valuable proposal for resolving this entire dilemma has been offered by the late Robert Hartman, who has studied Moore's ethics more carefully and with greater zest than anyone of whom I am aware. Recall Moore's denial that a substance is anything more than a concatenation of its natural properties. What does this resemble, if not Berkeley's rejection of the distinction between primary qualities (those alleged to inhere in an object) and secondary ones (those alleged to pertain to our perception of the object)? Sure, Moore is a realist--he parts company with Berkeley on that score. But the reduction of substances to their components can be plausibly aligned with Berkeley's reduction to phenomenal experience. As with the POU, what Berkeley is really objecting to is the assumption that the world comes (to us) in neat bundles. The division of a whole into its parts is a linguistic act, not a feat of ontological pre-packaging. (This makes Berkeley an ancestor of James. It also means that Moore's "refutation" of idealism in 1903 is tempered with appreciation for Berkeley's achievement. The latter accords with our thesis that Moore was capable of synthesizing contrasting world-views.) The danger of hypostatization is again the bugaboo; the primary-secondary distinction is harmless so long as it is not Platonized. Now what Hartman advances is that values are "tertiary qualities," which "...are to secondary qualities as secondary qualities are to primary qualities [Hartman (1981), 137, orig. in ital.]. This is not just picturesque langauge, but lends itself to precise reckoning: "the structure of value" for any given thing comprises "the set of its secondary properties" [Hartman (1967), 144, 2nd quote in ital. in orig.]. This explains at one stroke why, (i) we can verbally distinguish values from so-called descriptive properties, (ii) we can verbally distinguish so-called objective from subjective properties, while including values in the latter group, (iii) Moore insists that 'good' is found in things, yet is conceptually autonomous: non-empirical, yet not metaphysical (other-worldly). Its "nature" is logical, not ontological [Hartman (1981), 129], a thesis Moore struggled to express. Hence, the primary-secondary-tertiary distinction is reformulable in the language of set theory; it is a heuristic aid, to be replaced by mathematical comparisons among sets of different logical orders, of which value is always the highest one. Hence, we arrive at an axiological system which ranks "cardinalities of intentional sets" and defines 'good' as "...the set of all the intentional properties of a concept" [Hartman (1964-65), 256; his ital.].

Hartman's scope is breath-taking. Of course he preserves the insight that "the value predicate 'good'...is a property of concepts rather than of objects" [Hartman (1967), 103, orig. in ital.]. But he does much more. He shows how we need not be deterred by Moore's antique way of comparing (or contrasting) the ontological status of 'good' with that of natural objects. He provides a mathematically rigorous way of talking about values, which, if successful, lays to rest once and for all the charge that values are not fit subjects of knowledge. He strongly reinforces the thesis (compare pt. (a) on p. 41 above) that the set of "intrinsic natural properties" implies (because it abstractly constitutes) a value. He satisfies those who contend that values are "intangible," without conceding that they must "supervene on" or have no (logical) connection with facts. Best of all, he makes Moore's various assertions about goodness much less maddening to comprehend. In 1922, Moore maintains that intrinsic value "...depends solely on the intrinsic nature of the thing in question" [CIV, 260; orig. in ital.], or on "the intrinsic nature of what possesses it" [CIV, 273]. How can it so "depend," unless the f/v gap be bridged? Broad detected this ambiguity in 1942. Here is Moore's considered response:

XIV....if a thing is good, then that it is so _follows_ from the fact that it possesses certain natural intrinsic properties, which are such that from the fact that it is good it does _not_ follow conversely that it has those properties [PGEM, 588; M.s italics].

This isn't doubletalk; it is just Moore's way of distinguishing between sufficient and necessary conditions for good-making, respectively. But if allowing a one-way entailment between goodness and the possession of certain properties doesn't thoroughly compromise a f/v disjunction, nothing ever will. We should be overjoyed to find Moore contradicting his official platform, especially when we consider that he goes much further than our argument back in Chap. I that facts presuppose values would license. Yet, I am not happy, because Moore is not stupid, and I do not want to fall back on the lamest of all explanations of an author's statements- that Moore is nodding in his old age. One of Hartman's singular virtues is that he reconciles passages such as this with what Moore was getting at in PE, 39 years earlier. How? By the simple expedient of using Russellian type theory. The description of fact belongs to a different logical order than facts themselves. Likewise for valuation in relation to description. This is the tertiary-secondary-primary distinction all over again, but Hartman defends it in even quainter fashion: "As Being is to Fact, so X is to value. X is the highest value genus....There is a difference between genus and species of values" [Hartman (1967), 101-102]. Values are logical "transcendentals," and this is why the goodness of an object can follow from (or be strictly "dependent" upon) its having given properties, without in any way requiring us to identify 'good'(or value in general) as belonging to the same category as those properties. "Propositions about the intrinsic nature and about the intrinsic value of a thing are (extensionally, but never intensionally) equivalent" [Hartman (1967), 133, orig. in ital., parenthetical added]; this is what Moore was fighting for all along, even if he didn't hold it clearly or say it in an idiom that we (or his contemporaries) could follow.

Here at last is what we sought--a simultaneous explanation and vindication of the meaning of non-naturalism, one which does not compromise any of

Moore's discussions, spanning a period of four decades. Not only is Moore internally consistent, he was completely right! One can, therefore, forgive Hartman the mild extravagance of comparing Moore the axiologist to the most famous pioneers of modern science [Hartman (1967), 101, 147-149]. The Platonic "paradox of goodness" [Olthius (1968), 64]--that 'good' must somehow be real, yet cannot be articulated or tied to the world as we know it--has been solved [Hartman (1964-65), 256].

Before we ask whether Hartman has really accomplished all of this, let's digress for just a moment. Recall that at PE 41, Moore reintroduced the NF, in none other than its incarnation as the OQA. This is just one more sign of the central place which the OQA occupies in Moore's thought. Moore is undoubtedly right in criticizing those (e.g., sympathy theorists) who equate 'good' with a particular feeling. Indeed, the OQA isn't necessary for this purpose--Kant had several refutations handy. Tapping the results of introspection (he cannot conceive of 'good' as existing by itself in time, whereas he can conceive of many (unidentified) natural objects as doing so), though controversial, clearly foreshadows Moore's reliance on the method of isolation as the final (or sole) court of appeal both for valuation and value-theoretic construction, in PE Chap. VI. We may defer examining that until later. But there is one point we cannot bypass without immediate quarrel. If it can always be asked whether 'good' is X, why can't it be asked whether 'good' is (or ought to be) non-natural? If posing the OQA is unendingly intelligible, then specifying the "correct" ontology for values is an exercise in irrelevancy, no better than the Social Darwinism, historicism, hedonism or other pretentious doctrines that Moore deflates in PE Chaps. II-IV. A value treated as a fact is then guilty of what Moore calls the "supernaturalistic fallacy" [PE 125, 129]. Everything is what it is and not another thing--but why is it (good that it is) what it is? And (why) is it good that it is alleged to be good? The childish innocence (or nuisance) of the indefinitely iterated question [cf. p. 26] destroys the foundation, both of a naturalist and of a non-naturalist edifice. We must then fall back on the standard ploy, which regards 'non-natural' as a pejoratively non-referential term, a way of alluding, neither to what values are nor to what they aren't, but rather, to the inability (in principle) to justify any ontological program that tries to invoke them. If this dooms ontology to incompleteness, consider it another triumph for Goedel's ghost.

Sadly, this single point suffices to make Hartman's magnificent reconstruction fail. The OQA devastates value-theory, not just this or that conception of value. It is an equal opportunity destroyer. Value as distinct from fact, value as linked to fact; it undermines value on any construal. In the end, it demolishes itself: for we can always ask: (why) is the OQA good? Because we want or seek the truth? Why should we desire that? Because language entails some commitment to principles of order and rationality? [cf. Habermas (1971), 310, 314, and Aristotle, Metaphysics Bk IV 1005b34, 1007a20, 1008b5-7]. Then those principles must be defended without making tacit use of them, though avoidance of such circularity is manifestly impossible: as Strawson says, "We lack words to be able to say what it is to be without them" [Strawson (1966), 273]. Because knowledge is always useful? That one is hardly worth bothering to knock down. Because intellectual integrity demands it? [cf. Chap. I, esp. on page 10]. Then behold our primary norm, and we are launched on another regress. No matter which way we turn, we cannot escape. Luckily, neither can the OQA [Rohatyn (1982), 176]. If no argument is conclusively valid--indeed, if all arguments are conclusively invalid--then the OQA as a "metastandard" of argumentation is in exactly the same jeopardy, and so refutes itself.

Here, incidentally, is where the parallel between Moore and Goedel ends. While Goedel's incompleteness theorem does show that in any sufficiently rich formal system, a given (self-referential) proposition is (provably) unprovable, the theorem operates without causing logic any harm. The flickering counter-argument, that system $S + 1$ must be complete, because otherwise we could not know (prove) that S is incomplete, founders as soon as we recognize that the same predicament blocks $S + 1$, $S + 2$, and so on ad infinitum (cf. Alonzo Church's theorem, 1936). This is an unavoidable consequence of Goedel's own rules, or of extending the rules of Principia Mathematica so that "undecidability" crops up in the object-language of an infinite succession of axiomatic systems. Goedel's sentence G which says of itself 'G is unprovable' correctly deduces its own proof-failure, which is why it succeeds! The OQA is

not flexible in this way. It necessitates the
failure of all other value-theories, but not of
itself. And it is fair to call the OQA an incipient
value-theory. It is a sheer self-repeating question,
or a skeptical challenge which risks nothing, but
merely demands that a burden of proof or presumption
be met (which suffices to show too that no skeptic is
ever commitment-free). To demolish the OQA, we need
only make it its own target, vulnerable to self-
referential attack, whereas incompleteness among
formal systems does not make them unscientific, let
alone worthless. Someone might counter that the
failure of (e.g.) utilitarianism to justify its first
principles is likewise a grave defect. But we have
already discussed the false allure of the quest for
apodictic principles [Chap. V, pp. 26-27]. If a value
theory bogs or breaks down at any point, we are prone
to conclude that it has been entirely defeated. This
is not a rational estimate, or one that I subscribe
to; but it is a powerful urge which must be heeded.
If (e.g.) the rightness or wrongness of abortion
cannot be decided by appealing to (exclusively)
Kantian, utilitarian or some other principles, we do
not congratulate ourselves on how well these theories
work in less controversial areas. Too much is riding
on the existential issues for us to be smug, even for
a moment. Nor do we compare conflicting value-
theories to (say) wave-particle dualities in physics,
allowing one theory to "explain" one set of (non-
overlapping) data and another to "account for" the
rest. Our semi-conscious rationale is falsific-
ationist: if the theory should run into but one
counter-example that it cannot handle, it is
bankrupt, mistaken, dead. Of course, we do keep our
theories around, in the absence of replacements; but
they are not paradigms so much as object lessons, so
long as there is some war or terrorist act we cannot
justify (or repudiate), or even one human being whose
right to life we cannot invincibly establish (or
deny). Given these stakes, we are laudably hard on
ourselves. The OQA preys upon this sense of
intellectual guilt, and manipulates our need to be
sure by giving us the verdict we least expected, and
most feared. Only once we see that the charge of
question-begging can be turned against itself [cf.
Chap. I, pp. 6-7] can we free ourselves from the
self-torment that the OQA feeds upon.

A sympathetic critic of Moore might leap to his
defense and say, "Look, the OQA isn't what you make
it out to be. It's just a way of safeguarding

against the possibility of taking something for granted. It's meant to encourage us to bring our assumptions out into the open, to scrutinize them, rather than to conceal them or to pretend that they are air-tight. It is designed to prevent special pleading from masquerading as argument; it is not an indictment of arguments in general, or else it would indeed be self-spiteful." Now, I admit I am very sympathetic to the Popperian (and Millian) principle of fallibility as one of the foundations of any value-theory worth building. And I also think that it can survive self-referential criticism. Is fallibility fallible? Of course. Is it therefore false? No; this does not follow [cf. Bartley (1984), 224 ff.]. On the contrary, the assumption of fallibility is a presupposition of all attempts to criticize it; hence, any principle which supersedes it, must build upon or include it: an Aufhebung worthy of a naturalized Hegel. Popper misses a chance to make use of a neat transcendental argument; instead of capitalizing on the opportunity to show that fallibility is entailed by its own denial, he retreats to the safe yet sterile ground of differentiating between substantive and purely "methodological" proposals [Popper, "Replies To My Critics," in Schilpp (1974), Vol. II, 1010]. This linguistic device is shallow and unnecessary; it doesn't save Popper from inconsistency, but instead exhibits a rare failure of nerve on his part, preventing his philosophy from being complete in its embrace of incompleteness. We shall revert to this theme again in Chapter X (p. 107).

Despite my sympathy for fallibilism, it has only a limited bearing on Moore. If the OQA were intended to be a variant of fallibility, then there would be no further trouble; value-propositions would be endlessly corrigible in face of novel or unforeseen experience (including, dissenting opinions), and a vigorous scientific naturalism would be the fallibly regnant method for settling disputes and arriving at warranted value assertions. Can this be what Moore had in mind? If he did, then why all the fuss about the NF? Have our expositions been unnecessary, or in vain? Is Moore simply recommending that we play fair, then explicating fairness as showing our cards at all times, never bluffing? This is true, not trite, but how could anything so modest cause 80 years of frenzied philosophical controversy? Besides, this interpretation cannot bear the weight of Moore's frequent assertion that commission of the

NF is the biggest source of error in the history of ethics. True, Moore was no fan of dogmatism or intolerance; he detested a priori convictions, and one of his motives for propounding the OQA was to make us "...recognize that, so far as the meaning of good goes, anything whatever may be good," which makes deliberation "...start with a much more open mind" [PE 20]. But this sentence, for all its wisdom, throws us back upon the same dilemma as before: If "anything whatever may be good," then how is the "meaning of good" to be fixed or ascertained? (Again, Moore omits the single quotes necessary to distinguish 'good' from "the good".) Do goods have anything in common, in virtue of which we assign them that designation? Or is 'good' in one (non-natural) realm, while goods inhabit another? Of course, the phrase "anything whatever" refers to an opening stage of inquiry; but once we accept the OQA, we can never advance discussion, or get beyond that stage. One speculates that Moore, in his pedestrian and plodding way, translated the Nietzschean transvaluation of all values into Victorian prose, and took it even further than its "nihilist" progenitor ever dreamt. This is not to attribute to Nietzsche any overt, direct influence on Moore; but the road from Bern and Vienna to Cambridge is short and well-travelled, and the late 19th century correspondences are too great for coincidence.

In this discussion, poor Hartman has been left by the wayside! I claimed that the OQA defeats his masterly revision of Moore's text. But let's give Hartman a chance to speak for himself. He claims that his own stock of value principles "closes" the OQA [Hartman (1967), 120]. He defines 'x is a good C' as 'x has the properties of the intension of C.' This in turn implies that class-membership creates a 1-1 correspondence between the intension of C and the set of properties of x. This mapping means that the answer to the question "Is it good that x is a good C?" is simply yes, "...according to both the definition of 'x is a good C' and 'it is good that.'" Consequently, the OQA "...is passed by our axiom with flying colors" [Hartman (1967), 120]. Moore's only mistake was to regard 'good' as indefinable [Ibidem], but he is redeemed by his second thoughts on that subject [Ibid., 101]. Moore was unerringly right to resist "material" identification of Good with any object. Good is a "formal" concept, i.e., "...the logical procedure that makes anything good" [Ibid., 120]. This is in line with all of the earlier explications of 'good' as a second- (or third-) order concept, a set of sets (of sets). A contemporary author, without mentioning Hartman, nonetheless concurs with "the extreme generality of goodness" conceived as a "generic property" [Butcharov (1982), 64-65].

Quite apart from turning the NF into the accusation of an ontological category mistake, these ideas are unconvincing and dubious on other grounds. To start at the most obvious juncture: if the answer to the question "Is it good that x is a good C?" is yes, then (presumably) we have a right to ask "why?" On being told the answer, that this is a consequence of some initial stipulation, do I need to tell anyone what will happen next? Hartman tries to dodge the force of the OQA by interpreting it as a limited, rather than an unlimited, demand for justification. But this is a shallow ruse, which anyone can see through. All Hartman has done is to postpone having to defend his "conceptual" definition, while distorting the meaning and impact of the OQA in an effort to avoid trouble. If the OQA is as thorough as Moore intends, then restrictions of its scope are artificial and quite illegitimate. The NF loses its punch, so there is neither the possibility nor the need to make the OQA run afoul of itself. Value-theory is saved, but at the price of emasculating Moore's critique.

Hartman maneuvers in the same way when discussing ethical propositions as synthetic. He takes this to mean 'synthetic a priori'[Hartman (1964-65), 250], which is willful, to say the least. (A recent writer likewise claims that value-propositions must be synthetic a priori to count as "informative" [Hill (1976), 87], but fails to adduce any evidence that Moore was committed to this position, let alone that he understood himself in this way. Despite Moore's predilection for Kantian lingo [cf. Chap. V, p. 29 & Chap. VIII, p. 92], he cannot endorse a synthetic a priori line on value-propositions, since that would put them beyond logical criticism, and therefore violate the NF from version (1) (or a.) onward. The ascription of this view to Moore is therefore improper.) Granted this invention, Hartman freely creates a priori dicta. Good becomes "...the second-order property of the maximum intension possible" [Hartman (1967), 119; orig. in ital.]. Alternatively, "a thing is good insofar as it exemplifies its concept" [Ibid., 103, orig. in ital.]. What does this mean? Some philosophers [Neville (1981), 102-103] interpret this as Hartman's version of the principle of plenitude. If so, it gives rise to some familiar difficulties. For example, is Adolf Hitler good insofar as he fulfills the concept of Satanic evil? Is 3.14159 good insofar as it exemplifies pi? Or, is all of this just words?

To answer these objections, Hartman might begin by insisting that we rigorously specify the relevant concept in each case. For pi, it's the relation between the circumference of a circle and its diameter. Since 3.14159 does (nearly) exemplify that relation, yes, it is good. For Satanic evil, it's (e.g.) inflicting ingenious unrelenting horror on others. Hitler (unlike DeSade) did not do this imaginatively, hence, he does not fulfill the concept. Moreover, we should never confuse "good as Satanic" with "morally good," whether we are discussing weapons, policies or people. A good Nazi is a bad person; a good person would make a bad (or no) Nazi. Therefore, we must discriminate between, (a) a concept, (b) its substitution instances, (c) the criteria for employing the concept, (d) the correctness of those criteria, and (e) their (respective) justification or debatability.

As soon as we mount this defense, we rely implicitly on the OQA. Hence, we are back where we started. (My thanks go to the publisher's referee for stimulus on these issues.) After all, Hartman is Moore's witness, not his adversary. Hence, the novel ideas Hartman contributes are just excess baggage. He could never salvage Moore, even were he consistently faithful to Moore's principles. And Hartman's originality poses its own problems. For example, the "measurement" of value is a travesty of Moore's conception of non-natural objects, motivated by Hartman's construal of value hierarchies as a demonstrably orderly succession of Cantorian alephs! If nothing else, Hartman has a bold imagination for an ontologist. Of course, even if there were a Satanic prototype of which Hitler is a poor copy, what would the prototype be a prototype of? After 2,000 years, the 'third man' argument is still invincible, bagging Hartman as yet another victim of redundancy.

Despite its failure, Hartman's struggle to purify Moore is instructive. From it I infer that the only way to prevent the OQA from ridding us of

<u>value-theory is to rid it of itself</u>. And this cannot happen so long as we restrict it or apply it selectively to (un)favored contexts, but not across the board. For this reason, type theory is not permissible here. Clarifying "levels" of discourse would create a double standard, exempting the OQA from the force of its own strictures. By the OQA, this too is an arbitrary move. Type theory cannot rescue the OQA without destroying it (or itself).

I agree with John Hill that "Hartman's extraordinary conclusions are the result of an entirely false preconception of scientific philosophy" [Hill (1976), 27]. Yet Hill too maintains that for Moore, "Good...is undoubtedly a principle, but it is formal and vacuous: Moore's principles have the same function within ethics as the principles of logic have within that science" [Hill (1976), 31]. Suppose, just for argument's sake, that this were true; would anybody <u>want</u> to adopt Moore's principles as axiomatic? Going by PE Chap. I alone, value-theory would self-destruct. Nor will Chap. VI make matters easier for anyone with such ambitions, as we are about to discover. Moreover, Hill, like Hartman, contends that 'good' "...was metaethical, but only because it was metaphysical" [Hill (1976), 31]. Not only does this violate the OQA (including the specific objections against commission of the super-NF, in PE Chap. IV), it also requires its proponent to defend Platonism (or some near relative) as the correct interpretation of the status of (axio)logical laws. This is an additional burden, not to mention a gratuitous imposition on Moore's text.

In 1942, Moore exhibited his distaste for formalization. Responding to a paper by Abraham Edel, Moore flatly rejected any attempt to formulate his value-theories in a Euclidean mold [PGEM 620-623]. But this does not disturb me. Despite his friendship with Russell, Moore was untouched by the new logic. Although he was never temperamentally opposed to symbolization, he made little use of such techniques himself. His resistance to Edel may have been due to relative unfamiliarity with discussions couched in that form. The goal of Edel's discussion is to show that Moore himself commits the NF by conceiving 'good' as the object of a special kind of beholding [PGEM 161]. If that is so, then axiomatization likewise reaches a dead end, in this case thanks to the bankruptcy of Intuition as a cognitive mode [cf. Chapter VII, pp. 64-65]. Even if Hill and especially Hartman manage to avoid self-invalidation on this front, the OQA renews the threat, making the demise of value-theory imminent. Logic is a wonderful tool, but it cannot change or improve principles that are hopelessly extreme or perverse from the start. The unqualified application of the OQA falls into the same trap as (say) Russell's paradox. It is indeed fortunate that some ideas slay themselves, before they can slaughter their fellows.

Despite my criticisms of Hartman, I greatly respect what he has done to advance the cause of interpreting Moore as a systematic ethician, imbued with a slippery yet unified world-view. Hartman makes us respect Moore as not just a poser of formidable barriers or a repository of scattered, desultory attempts to hurdle them. He has helped and compelled me to consolidate my own exegeses, not least when they are in opposition to his. And his limitless fondness for Moore's writings was a rarity in an age which tended to praise Moore without studying PE carefully. However, we cannot refrain from drawing the obvious conclusion that flows from Moore's own pronouncements. "If we ask: What bearing can Metaphysics have upon the question, What is good? the only possible answer is: Obviously and absolutely none" [PE 118; M.s capitals]. Later (Chapter IX), we shall discover ways to reverse this judgment, using Moore's own texts to undermine its force. The claim that "...Metaphysics...can have no logical bearing whatever upon...the fundamental ethical question 'What is good in itself?'" [PE 139-140; M.s capitals) will not survive intense scrutiny. But for now, we will accede to Moore's verdict that metaphysics is irrelevant to value--both to the determination of intrinsic value and to the resolution of the underlying meaning of 'good.' Hence, ontology cannot support one value thesis as opposed to some other. Besides, if the OQA is sound, all attempts to ground value in an ontology are equally fallacious. This is the Goedelian analogy with a vengeance. Moore conveys the message again in PE Chap. IV, when he dismisses Kant's notion of pure will [PE 127], and a number of other (metaphysical) principles.

Appearances can be deceiving. Moore always rehearses what look like the same arguments, yet on closer inspection they have several distinct strands.

Through it all, he remains quite unaware of their density and complexity. What for him was a single thought actually involves a network of interrelated ideas. The naturalistic fallacy is a Gestalt, a unity amidst multiplicity, the one (OQA) pervading the many.

CHAPTER VII

A SECOND TOUR: PRINCIPIA ETHICA (PE), CHAPTER VI

Round 1: The Real vs. The Not So Ideal

Up to now we have been following Moore's own topical progression in examining the contents of PE. Now it is time to depart from that format. PE Chap. VI must be introduced ahead of PE Chap. V, for reasons that can only become clear as the story unfolds. I will begin with the (best remembered) quotation from Moore's concluding chapter on "The Ideal":

> XV. By far the most valuable things, which we know or can imagine, are certain states of consciousness, which may roughly be described as the pleasures of human intercourse and the enjoyment of beautiful objects [PE 188].

Passages such as this were what presumably led Keynes and other Bloomsburians to idolize Moore as "better than Plato" [for Keynes' second thoughts, see Levi (1974), 185-186]. Maybe he was better, although you couldn't prove it by my students. Whenever we read XV in class, someone invariably challenges me as follows: Why couldn't the ideal consist of guzzling beer 24 hours a day? My first response is to cite Moore's appropriation of Plato's Philebus [PE 88-89], which distinguishes between mere pleasure and the consciousness necessary to heighten and intensify it. Incidentally, this is one of the few favorable judgments Moore made about another author [cf. PE 17, on Sidgwick's anticipation of the NF]. A nonstop beer drinker quickly (or eventually) becomes comatose. What then? My students don't find this objection convincing. (1) Moore doesn't say the "most valuable things" have to be enduring. Couldn't the short, happy life of Francis Beachcomber rate higher on the value-scale than 50 years of reading poetry by candlelight or gazing at Grecian urns? (2) Why not live and let live--different value-strokes for differently evaluating folks? Why the need to pronounce universal judgments, which is just a disguised polemic on behalf of social or class conformity? (3) Why is consciousness such a worthwhile addition to an experience? Why not unconsciousness? Perhaps the drunk lying in a

drunken stupor is enjoying life more than those who
are awake can ever do (this is not a frivolous
proposal; consider right-to-life claims for
permanently unconscious individuals, those who
function solely thanks to biological support
systems).

These objections are well-taken. If you think
not, try rebutting them and see what happens.
Besides, what are "the pleasures of human intercourse
and the enjoyment of beautiful objects?" Friendship
and art? Sex and art? Friendship and sex? When we
try to guess just what Moore had in mind, the
plausibility of taking exception to his narrow
outlook grows, unless we apply the 'criterion of
sufficient vagueness' (a phrase coined by Professor
Dennis Temple) to XV. Moore doesn't itemize what
objects and relations qualify as beautiful and
friendly. Hence even the Manson family might agree
with the general formula for summa bona, no matter
how divergent or eyebrow-raising their applications
of it might be. Nor do the conceptual problems end
there. Moore justifies his choices by an appeal to
consensus: "No one, probably, who has asked himself
the question, has ever doubted that personal
affection and the appreciation of what is beautiful
in Art or Nature, are good in themselves; nor, if we
consider strictly what things are worth having purely
for their own sakes, does it appear probable that any
one will think that anything else has nearly so great
a value" [PE 188-189, M.s italics]. Apart from
whether Moore's data-sampling is reliable, this is a
flagrant ad populum argument. After several chapters
of having our noses rubbed in fallacies, it is a
pleasure, albeit a malicious one, to find fault with
Moore on the same score. Better than Plato? Not
this; not on Plato's worst days, of which there were
very few.

There is another difficulty surrounding Moore's
insistence that "...personal affections and aesthetic
enjoyments include all the greatest, and by far the
greatest, goods that we can imagine..." [PE 189, M.s
italics]. Moore calls these the reason for virtue's
being: "...it is only for the sake of these things-
in order that as much of them as possible may at some
time exist-that anyone can be justified in performing
any public or private duty..." [PE 189]. These summa
bona "...form the rationale ultimate end of human
action and the sole criterion of social progress..."
[PE 189]. Them's fighting words, and music to a

Woolf's ears [Levy (1979), 253-259 traces the abortive movement to persuade Moore to produce a "manifesto"]. But if we have read PE Chap. V, they will also sound very odd. There, Moore defines (sic) duty as doing "...that action, which will cause more good to exist in the Universe than any possible alternative" [PE 148]. He ponders the implications of this formulation of 'ideal utilitarianism,' whose key word is "possible." Since we must compare alternative lines of conduct into an indefinite future, "...our causal knowledge along is far too incomplete for us ever to assure ourselves..." [PE 149] that what we are (or propose) doing is the right thing. So "...it follows that we never have any reason to suppose that an action is our duty; we can never be sure that any action will produce the greatest value possible" [PE 149]. Moore does not hesitate to draw the conservative conclusion that it is unwise to advocate "changes in social custom," since "...it seems doubtful whether Ethics can establish the utility of any rules other than those generally practiced" [PE 161].

The PE Chap. V recommendations are pure sophistry. Theoretical doubt is one thing; practical doubt is another--Locke and Peirce, among others, have stressed the relevant differences. This is one more respect in which Moore plays (and preys) upon the agent's felt need for certainty, which is an unrealistic but all too understandable program. It is a sign, too, that Moore is not a fallibilist [cf. pp. 47-49). No fallibilist goes from the undeniable premise that we can and do make mistakes, to the conclusion that we should do nothing or remain paralyzed. To the contrary: unless we take risks, then, as James and Popper both urge, we cannot even discover our errors. But this is an aside. We don't expect Moore to take a bold stand in PE Chap. VI, given the express timidity of PE Chap. V. If we can never know or be sure of our duties, how can we ever determine the relation between duty as a means and some allegedly ultimate end? Seen in context, Moore's categorical stance is far more shocking and unexpected than anything that precedes its appearance. Forget about disagreement over lifestyles or preferred activities, or Moore's tenuous logic in backing up these recommendations. PE Chaps. I-IV inform us that value-theory is both inherently and historically defective; Chapter V purports to tell us that value-practice is incapable of making trustworthy predictions or of finding anything except general rules of thumb by which to guide ordinary decision-making [PE 155]. By Chapter VI, the overall prospects are pretty grim. More than anything else, quote XV comes as a complete surprise, a reversal of form. It is uncharacteristic optimism, coming from a thinker who has carefully and suspensefully steeled us for the opposite. From the beginning, when we are told that "...good is good, and that is the end of the matter" [PE 6], we learn not to find Moore's laconic creeds "disappointing." After five chapters of assessing the tradition as bankrupt, we are not ready for such an abrupt about-face.

Moore proves his elusiveness a second time, in Ethics. After distinguishing between whether an action is right or wrong and whether one can (n)ever know this [E 53], Moore goes on to consider whether "disobedience would be wrong" [E 76] in case it, as opposed to compliance with an established rule, were to maximize well-being or utility in a given case. Although "we hardly ever, if ever, know for certain which among the courses open to us will produce the best consequences" [E 81, M.s italics], Moore holds (despite several objections that he brings up himself) that "...right and wrong depend on the actual consequences of an action" [E 81, M.s italics], not on foreseen, probable, or ideal effects. So a person "...absolutely ought to choose the course, which he has reason to think will be the best" [E 82, M.s italics]. Should events turn out otherwise, (s)he is not automatically blameworthy [E 81]. Conversely, since a malicious soul may, through stupidity or miscalculation, augment rather than decrease goodness, Moore is cheerfully "...committed to the paradox that a man may really deserve the strongest moral condemnation for choosing an action, which actually is right" [E 82, M.s italics]. Aristotle recognized long ago that we sometimes act against belief, not just desire [Nicomachean Ethics, Bk VII, Chapter 3, 1146b28-30, 1147a3, a36] and that even vicious (wo)men make errors that are felicitous. Bad desires are not only possible [PE 67], they can even turn out well, if not for the agent then for everyone else who may be affected by the resulting action. This isn't a "paradox," or difficult to reconcile with the stated principle that actual consequences are the test of right and wrong. What is courageous is that Moore's verdict overturns the PE Chapter V analysis. Since actual consequences are the test of fulfilling one's duty, then, despite the incurable hazard that no one can tell "beforehand" how an action will turn out [E 82], performance becomes mandatory, notwithstanding the absence of reliable rules to guide us. Like an existentialist staring down the abyss of unfounded choice, Moore forces the agent to move off center, to legislate the will, calmed only by the small reassurance that judgments of personal worth will canvass intention, and not be based on execution alone.

The simplest explanation of this development is that Moore changed his mind between 1903 and 1912. This accords with Moore's twin reputation for modesty and honesty. But, we cannot assume that the later reformulation is a conscious retraction of Moore's older conception of obligation, for the simple reason that he makes no mention of what he averred in PE. Hence, one cannot be sure whether Moore's flexibility is due to Socratic self-effacement or some other cause. Also, while Moore defends the "...actual consequences or results" doctrine [E 72, M.s italics] from the outset of his 1912 discussion, he does not say why, though he does dispose of alternatives by elimination. (Point-by-point comparison and contrast between PE and Ethics would be very worthwhile, though it will not be undertaken here.)

It is tempting to search out other explanations of the disparity between PE Chap. V and VI. As an English gentleman, defending the status quo must have come naturally! The two chapters are perfectly consistent in this regard. The first tells you never to rebel against authority, while the second rebels in the only way that is left: via aesthetic escape and the forgoing of private, as opposed to public, bonds. And even such sanctuary as this affords is the prerogative of an elite caste, those with money, education, manners, social standing and whatever additional resources may be required. Moore is nothing, then, if not an Establishment type, for whom "...abstract, technological rationality has its sociological meaning. Principia Ethica too has its pretensions to impersonality,...and yet no work in contemporary philosophy could be more clearly interpreted as an unconscious repository of social values" [Levi (1974), 280]. On the other hand, at his best Moore is just the opposite. In PE Chap. II, he criticizes those who (e.g.) feign to equate 'good' with what is natural or normal. Rhetorically, he asks "was the excellence of Socrates or of Shakespeare normal? Was it not rather abnormal, extraordinary?" [PE 43]. Against Herbert Spencer, he quietly but cuttingly notices that the evolutionary survival of the "higher" races meant, as in the case of Native Americans, that "we can kill them more easily than they can kill us" [PE 47]. Of course, these are stock examples, not Moore's invention or his literary property. And they are somewhat removed from the specific situations which were or should have been agonizing for an Edwardian in 1903. Nonetheless, Moore is no authoritarian, and the NF hardly gives aid or comfort to any of the -isms, ideologies or racial doctrines which have sprouted in this century. (Its effect would be salutary, if only it didn't "disprove" so much.)

As Levi astutely observed, PE exhibits "...a profound conflict between a bourgeois and conservative conformity to social rules and the glimmerings of aesthetic revolt..." [Levi (1974), 312], which will occupy us again later. For now, it is pertinent that Moore's anti-naturalism, rather than a disposition to turn then-current institutions and avant-garde iconoclasms into the bearers of eternal verities, is responsible for tying his hands. PE Chap. II can support a Thoreau, Gandhi or King in their respective struggles against injustice. PE Chap. V meekly reduces the individual to ineffectiveness: anything (s)he can do is likely not to become a general practice anyway [PE 161], and even if they succeed, any policy, new or old, must be well-nigh universal before it can claim a prima-facie hold on future actions [PE 181]. Moore's misguidedly principled refusal to make use of empirical facts or scientific techniques is responsible for these inadvertent but shameful concessions to City Hall. Yet, even amidst the illicit conversion of the actual into the unalterable, Moore resists complete fetishization. He characteristically warns against confusing means, "...what seems absolutely necessary here and now, for the existence of anything good..." with the genuine ends ("good in itself") which means are supposed to subtend [PE 187]. This isn't applied as broadly as it should be, and it never causes Moore to review his Chapter V attitudes. But I attribute this to blindness, not philistinism. As we have already noted, Moore is in the embarrassing position (especially for a philosopher) of not knowing himself very well. Why should Chapter V cohere with Chapter VI, when it doesn't even fit with Chapter II? Moore's complexity (or his sheer contradictoriness) runs away with him at times.

There is no reason to gloat about this; sooner or later, it happens to us all. Nor is there any reason to be despondent. Like many thinkers, Moore often does his best and most rewarding work while under the influence of conflicting models of what the world is like. It is to his (or his daimon's) credit that he does not willfully suppress one set of insights in favor of another, just to achieve a foolish consistency. Our examination of the NF revealed that approaches which (temporarily) make Moore look muddled are preferable to those which reduce him to a single formula. You may protest: doesn't the OQA as we interpreted it serve as just such a device? Oh yes. But if it were Moore's last (or only) word, could Chapter VI of PE ever have been composed? The study of Moore is a bacchanalian revel, which defeats the most meticulous, while defying the intellectual sobriety of its source.

Round 2: **Possible Worlds vs. Actual Agents**

Moore doesn't just arrive at his MVPs (most valuable pleasures) by legerdemain. He announces them shortly after introducing the "method of absolute isolation" [PE 188] and reintegrating the principle of organic unities (POU) into the work [PE 187]. Moore maintains that XV is the direct outcome of applying the isolation test, to generate a solution to age-old "controversies of Ethics" [PE 188]. Moreover, the second clause of XV's first sentence ("which we know or can imagine") suggests that Moore has introspectively discovered the cardinal value truths which he states thereafter. It is therefore high time to look into the isolation test (IT) in earnest, since without it Moore lacks a basis for many of his subsequent assertions, save for what flaccid appeals to public opinion might gain him.

The IT provides the method whereby to render a judgment about the intrinsic value of any (real or proposed) item. Moore alludes to the concept of intrinsic value very early on [PE 17], in the course of trying to explain what 'good' as a "non-natural" object must be. We still intend to defer explication of the meaning of 'intrinsic value' for as long as possible. Luckily, the IT allows us to do this, since it concerns the extension rather than the intension of the concept. An IT determines what has value, and to what "degrees." It therefore presupposes, but need not make explicit, a logically prior understanding of what 'intrinsic value' is. For to judge that X is good, "...is surely to judge whether the universal property of which it is an instance is (a) good" [Butcharov (1982), 66, his parentheses]. But this does not require us to lay out the criteria of goodness, any more than acts of perception require us to set forth the criteria for having a perception, or for (re)identifying objects in the perceptual field. It is the philosopher's task to explain what an <u>it</u> does. Whereas, it is the user's task to employ it, in order to:

XVI....consider what things are such that, if they existed by <u>themselves</u>, in absolute isolation, we should yet judge their existence to be good [PE 187, M.s italics].

The philosopher has just explained what the test is, and how to use it. Or has he? Just what does "absolute isolation" mean? This phrase has occasioned much misunderstanding. An early commentator held that the very phrase was non-sensical, since nothing (exempting God) can exist in complete isolation from other objects. Hence, the test was denounced as meaningless and, therefore, worthless [Roberts (1941), 624-625]. This scores a verbal victory, but it hardly does justice to Moore's admittedly obscure intention. "Isolation" is indeed impossible to achieve. Suppose, angered by high gasoline prices, I dream of a world without petroleum. Now in a world without petroleum, what else must be removed, retooled, or given up? Combustion engines, of course. Fossils, possibly. And myriad other items. There is never such a thing as the world minus only one item, since so many items are (causally or else logically) interconnected. But is <u>everything</u> interconnected, as the Hegelian school claimed? If so, then isolation tests would indeed be chimerical. Small wonder that Moore had to deny Idealism to make room for value. Fortunately, as we saw on pp. 34-36, complete interconnection would make it impossible to distinguish between parts and wholes. The universe would reduce to a single, Parmenidean entity about which rational--or any--discourse would be perforce limited. Everything is what it is and not another thing--but there is more than one thing! Wholes are wholes, parts are parts, but there is a plurality of both. No matter how large a unit is, it is always distinguishable from something else, unless we are bucking for an antinomy. The term "isolation" appears to set the bounds of size or inclusiveness too low, but it is likewise fallacious to set them too high. Note that this entire analysis is based on strictly semantic considerations; it does not assume the correctness of Moore's account of value. Moore can therefore concede that "isolation" is a figure of speech, that a multiplicity of factors is always involved, whether we are judging automobiles, Vermeers, or peace vs. war. His position is untarnished, indeed enhanced, once we take 'isolation' as a metaphor or abbreviation for a more intricate process of gestalt-like discrimination.

Moore's eschewal of 'good' conceived as a complex whole [PE 15] may have something to do with the unfortunate tendency to take him at his word. But as we get to know PE, we begin to make allowances for Moore's slovenly and at the same time wooden vocabulary. We begin to appreciate his struggle to express his most novel points in language that could not have come easily to him, or anyone else. To gain an understanding that isolation isn't quite what it seems, we need only return our attention to the POU. Moore emphasizes that a part of a given whole can (routinely, if not dramatically) and does have a different value from the whole(s) to which it attaches or belongs. Moore offers further examples of such contextuality. The value of pleasure "existing absolutely by itself" [PE 188, orig. in ital.] is, minus consciousness, negligible, exactly as Plato argued. So is a goal such as self-realization, considered apart from what does the realizing (and vice versa). These examples demonstrate the soundness of the POU. They also show why Moore connects the POU with the IT. If values can and do vary as a function of context, then there must be an underlying law or principle which admits and accounts for such variation. Acceptance of the POU commits us (in Moore's eyes) to the IT, since the latter brings out latent features of the former. "The principle of organic unities is itself established by the help of the method of isolation" [Duncan-Jones (1957), repr. in Ambrose and Lazerowitz (1970), 313]. Hints about this are dropped early on [PE 35, 93], belying my unconventional wisdom that Moore always performs about-faces. Not this time; PE Chap. VI just brings the IT into the open. Here we do not have to strain to achieve a unified understanding of the text; it is present from the start. But none of this sheds any light on the original problem, which is to elucidate the phrase "absolute isolation." We have an inkling of what it does not mean; can we offer some positive reflections on what it connotes?

Two related, mutually compatible construals suggest themselves. One is that an IT is in effect the creation of a possible world (PW). Leibniz, and more recently Kripke, have made it fashionable to think along such lines. Thus, if I am asked whether the world is (or would be) better off without prunes, I am in effect comparing two PWs: one, a world (such as ours) with prunes, the other a world minus this fruit or its chemical and nutritional equivalent. It is then up to me to judge the relative merits of both (or all) worlds, and to render a verdict. If the comparison involves n̄ possible worlds, then (for completeness' sake) it is necessary to rank them hierarchically. Since Moore doesn't tell us a great deal about it, I am left to suppose that once an IT is properly constructed, the answers to the questions it raises about the relative merits of each of two or more PWs will become self-explanatory. How else are we to understand yet another vexing passage from PE Chap. V which bears upon this issue? Here, Moore distinguishes between Intuition and having (or giving) reasons for one's assertions. An Intuition never has any reasons behind it, "except itself alone." Intuitions are "a sufficient reason" for themselves, but Moore, realizing that he is in danger of equivocating, quickly remonstrates that Intuition is never "an alternative to reasoning" [PE 144]. Instead, we must recognize that "nothing whatever can take the place of reasons for the truth of any proposition; intuition can only furnish a reason (in a quasi-sense) for holding any proposition to be true...when any proposition is self-evident, when...there are no reasons which prove its truth" [PE 144, M.s italics, parenthetical added].

The reader can spot all sorts of problems here. Could Intuition be wrong? Yes (Moore doesn't deny it). Then what good is it as a method of discovery, let alone of justification? If it is valid, doesn't that show that the unprovability of first principles of value is in exactly the same condition as the axioms of logic, arithmetic or geometry--just as Aristotle and Euclid (among others) supposed? And what about the OQA--doesn't it rout any attempt to smuggle in introspection, issuing self-justifying propositions (NF, in versions (10), f. and g.)? Why is Moore even bothering to draw on Intuition, except as an oversight or a failure of logical nerve, i.e., inability to face the devastation of value-theory brought to light in PE Chap. I? Later, I will add one more dilemma to this list. For now, let's not dwell on these shortcomings. The PW construal has one advantage which could not have escaped Moore's early devotees: it captures the standpoint of the artist who is engaged in creating something new. Every painter, sculptor, composer, poet or writer must ask themselves: Is what I am making really a beneficial addition to the world's stock of events and entities? Will it make the world better (more beautiful), or proliferate evil, ugliness or junk? I encounter this problem in deciding whether to write, revise or publish (every draft of each page of) this book. Yahweh, Plato's demiurge, Whitehead's God, all decide in their different ways what to exclude or include. Some start from scratch (ex nihilo), some from pre-existent matter, utilizing categories from among which a selection of contingencies must be made. They are artists too, experiencing at once the exhilaration and the responsibility of making a new beginning, even in the face of material or logical constraints. This must be what real freedom tastes like: a combination of sensitivity, a sense of order, power and self-restraint, coupled with the resolve, not to squander or destroy the precious and irreversible opportunity that life presents. This is what led Kant to find in art the symbol of morality: the self-imposed norm, the wedding between freedom and necessity through rationality, the creation of "purposefully purposeless" works, tangible products of our intangible and mutual respect for persons as ends in themselves. When I read Moore, I cannot help but feel that he echoes Kant's Critique of Judgment in his own way. (Nietzsche's Zarathustra isn't so far away, either, except that he only respects fellow artists.)

These reflections bring us to the second, complementary construal of the IT. Since we are all creators insofar as we make and raise children, transform the environment to suit human needs, and arrange forms of (social) self-government, it is not just God, the artist or the exceptional person who faces decisions for which a PW analysis is desirable or illuminating. We all have to. We must spectate time and eternity, to make a decision about the here and now. This isn't misplaced grandiloquence, or a

metaphysical rhapsody. While the decisions we make
may not be as fateful or catastrophic as (say) the
dropping of the atomic bomb on Hiroshima, they can be
just as permanent in their consequences. (Plato knew
this, both in portraying Alcibiades in Symposium and
in relating the Myth of Er which climaxes the
Republic.) These considerations, rather than any
literalist interpretations of the referents of "non-
natural objects," earn Moore the right to be
(favorably) compared with someone like Kant or Plato.
Moore drastically underestimates the factors involved
in making decisions; true to his earliest promise [PE
4-5] he offers no assistance when it comes to the
business of casuistry, of making hard personal (or
institutional) choices. But the gravity, the
significance of such situations, and what they entail
about being human, are not lost on him at all. His
early admirers were right to be enchanted by this.
The fact that they all belonged to a certain class of
literati does not negate what they saw, or make its
scope less universal, for precisely the reasons that
we have given. Perhaps this even explains why in PE
Chap. V Moore froze when confronted with the modal
variables affecting choice. In retrospect, his
cautionary remarks appear sane and sensible, rather
than rear-guard and reactionary. Did (e.g.) the
Bolshevik revolution create a better world, or only a
blood-bath? If Marx had it to do all over again,
armed with clairvoyance, would he have disseminated
the Manifesto, or Capital? Would Lenin have let
Stalin become his political heir? What about
Einstein, Fermi, Oppenheimer and the atomic bomb?
And so on. The magnitude of either/or situations can
be most calmly and serenely faced in art, which is
one reason for the tone of relative detachment heard
in PE Chap. VI. But don't be misled. Art is not a
form of escape, and neither is aesthetics. Both are
microcosmic representations of the profundity of
agency. The possible world semantics developed by
modal logicians is the a priori counterpart of the
existential predicament. Hegel is still smiling down
at us.

A possible world is an array of hypothetical
conditions a--n. The isolation test evaluates these,
either by themselves or in relation to one or more
alternative arrays a1--n1, a2--n2, and so on. The
testers are at liberty to alter the conditions of the
thought experiment at will, including (if they wish)
to insert or remove themselves from the list of
hypotheses to be judged. The criterion for conducting

the test, i.e., ranking the value of the worlds, remains a mystery, or is in the eyes of their beholders.

Round 3: And Still a Fallacy!

1. At PE 201, Moore defines 'beauty'. Yes, defines. The beautiful is "...that of which the admiring contemplating is good in itself." He prefaces this with the sweeping claim that "the naturalistic fallacy has been quite as commonly committed with regard to beauty as with regard to good: Its use has introduced as many errors into Aesthetics as into Ethics" [M.s capitals]. A few pages later, Moore repeats the very same definition, while adding one for 'ugly': "...that of which the admiring contemplation is evil in itself" [PE 208]. Wait, there is more:

2. In PE Chap. I, Moore warned against confusing "two natural objects with one another," or a natural object with a non-natural one [PE 13]. Here are two non-natural objects: 'good' and 'beauty'. Doesn't the same moral apply? Evidently not. Granted, there are "...two <u>different</u> objective predicates of value" [PE 201, M.s italics], but "...so related to one another that whatever is beautiful is also good" [PE 201]. Extensional equivalence aside, intensional differences remain. (a) 'Good' is the sole "<u>unanlysable</u> predicate of value." (b) 'Beauty' is "not identical with" 'good.' However, (c) 'Beauty is analysable; it is "defined by reference" to 'good'. This insures that (d) beauty and goodness are both "different from and necessarily connected with" one another [PE 201-202, M.s italics], reminiscent of the Greek notion of <u>Kalon</u>. Unanalyzability of 'good' is a corollary of its logical simplicity, following up on Moore's Chapter I gloss: "It is one of those innumerable objects of thought which are themselves incapable of definition, because they are the ultimate terms by reference to which whatever <u>is</u> capable of definition must be defined [PE 9-10, M.s italics]. 'Beauty' is subordinate to 'good', like the relation between 'straight line' and 'point' in Euclidean geometry.

3. One's first encounter with these passages is bound to be stunning. What, Moore, the great proponent of indefinability, defining what beauty is? For a long time I used to think that Moore was guilty

of a serious inconsistency [cf. Rohatyn (1982), 178]. But as the analysis on pp. 29-31 showed, in delineating the NF indefinability is at best a secondary, perhaps even a negligible consideration. Even versions (5) and (6) of the original list are comparatively safe. Moore allows you to compare two items, provided you don't equate them. Beauty and goodness are distinct; their extensions overlap, but their intensions are as different as Frege's celebrated 'morning star' and 'evening star'. It is only the grip of the textbook Moore (cf. p. 19) which misleads us into supposing that something is amiss.

But let's not be too hasty in dismissing the worry. For if no two concepts may be equated, how do we ever manage to define anything? Since synonyms are ruled out, does this force us to use Intuition over and over, creating a series of discrete objects of contemplation? If so, then Frankena's assessment that Moore's entire approach "...is as useless as an English butcher in a world without sheep" (is vindicated [Frankena (1939), repr. in Klemke (1969), 38]. Science surely couldn't operate this way, and even if (by hypothesis) people didn't disagree, how could they communicate their Intuitions to each other? The alternative is to say that Moore isn't serious about precluding identities. After all, he defines beauty in terms of goodness, doesn't he? While this is a tacit case of class-inclusion, so are the tedious examples paraded before us in Chapter I [PE 7,31]. More striking is Moore's dalliance with the referents of 'good' in that chapter. There, 'intrinsic value', 'intrinsic worth' and the judgment that a thing 'ought to exist' are all accorded interchangeable status [PE 17]. I am skeptical about the last of these, as there may be cases in which something ought to exist even though it has no intrinsic merit, e.g., an effective complaint bureau for citizens of Orwell's Oceania, or a single tool which will fix whatever is wrong with my car. While mutual substitutability is not synonymy, in these cases it is suspiciously close.

4. At this point, I want to wave a wand and make (in)definability go away. It is boring, overworked, and enough to make operationalists of us all. Luckily it is not essential to the NF, thanks to the OQA. Whether Moore is justified in saying that the NF has been "commonly committed" [PE 201] is quite another story. He seems to have in mind theories such as the Thomistic [S.T., Ia, 5,4, ad 1] which define beauty

as 'that which when seen pleases us.' This bothers Moore, because he wants aesthetic (as much as ethical) judgments to be objective. He returns to this theme in 1922, arguing that there is a deep cleavage between those who would defend the conception of intrinsic value and those who, while rejecting it, also reject subjectivist accounts of value [CIV, 258-259]. Whether aesthetic judgments are objective or not, Moore ought to know better than to circumvent the problem by replacing somebody else's definition with his own--which is exactly what he does, to insure that the resulting propositions will be capable of truth or falsity. This maneuver <u>does</u> commit the NF (versions (8), (10), (12), e., f., g., and h.), which explains why we cannot weasel Moore out of it, or suppress our discomfort when reviewing Moore's tactics.

The NF is safe. It was never in jeopardy, since it concerns, not words but their misuse in the conduct of argument. However, Moore is vulnerable to the NF. He tumbles into his own booby-trap, a victim of his own logical defenses. This invalidates, not the NF but the "definition" of beauty which evades and hides from its adversaries. Like many another philosopher who failed to heed one of his own warnings, Moore can admonish us to do as he says, not as he does. But this is only the beginning of a long and arduous intellectual journey.

Route 4:   Knowledge and Beauty

Having told us that "the enjoyment of beautiful objects" [PE 188] is one of the two chief goods that makes life worthwhile, it is not surprising that Moore attempts to define beauty, even if his definition violates a prior standard that he imposed. Granting that aesthetic experience is valuable, the relevant questions are, what makes it valuable? What makes aesthetic experience "aesthetic" in quality? Moore starts out by examining the respective contributions demanded from object and subject. The object must be beautiful; it must possess all those properties, qualities and relations in virtue of which such assessment is or would be just. But the agent or subject must, (i) perceive the work, (ii) know that it is perceiving the work, (iii) perceive the work as beautiful, (iv) know that it is perceiving the work as beautiful, (v) perceive (know that) the work is beautiful for the right reasons, i.e., those rules pertaining to correct aesthetic

assessment in general, applied to the judgment of
this work in particular, and (vi) have the proper
emotion or feeling towards this work, in light of
criteria (i)-(v). (This list does not claim to be
exhaustive, but for argument's sake, we will assume
its accuracy. It summarizes the "three different
cases" which Moore analyzes at PE 193.)

    These logical conditions for the ascription of
the term 'aesthetic' to an experience are far too
abstract to be of assistance in pronouncing judgment
on a Rembrandt painting or a Beethoven symphony. Nor
are they meant to be practical. Rather, they define
what a connoisseur is. They enable Moore to
distinguish between what he calls an "error of
judgment" and an "error of taste" [PE 192]. If I am
high on LSD and imagine I am confronting a Goya, I
commit the former mistake. If I am confronting a
Goya but am unmoved, or prefer to look at a Warhol, I
commit the latter. Since genuine aesthetic
experience occurs only when all six criteria are
fulfilled, there are many permutations which may fall
short of the ideal, yet are intriguing in some way.
Here's a scenario. Suppose that I dream that I am in
the Norton Simon museum, staring at a Degas. Does
this count as a genuine perception? Presumably not,
since my eyes are closed. Does it nonetheless count
as knowledge? There is no Degas hanging in my living
room, nor am I seeing the one in the museum. Yet the
one I am "seeking" in my dream is "really" there. I
may be under the (temporary) misapprehension that I
am seeing it in the museum, but I am not under any
misapprehension as to what I am "seeing". During the
dream, someone may "question" me and I may
"mistakenly" tell them 'that's a Van Gogh.' Nor is
my "knowledge" limited to dream-state facts. Suppose
that in my dream I also linger over a Van Gogh,
pronounce it the artistic equal of a Goya or a
Rembrandt, and hold it far superior to anything that
Warhol has ever done. Suppose, too, that I
vicariously experience the same elevation of mood as
the connoisseur seeing the painting in Pasadena might
do. Doesn't this qualify, or at least come close to
fulfilling all of the six conditions that Moore lays
out? If not, isn't it at least higher on the
adequacy scale than (say) the judgment of an awake
philistine?

    Moore doesn't wade through such muddy cases.
Nor does he rank the relative weight of any of the
proffered criteria, which would enable us to decide

them for ourselves. (But see pp. 74-77 below, for Moore's examination of real vs. imaginary evils.) He does insist that subjectivity plays a role in any aesthetic experience worthy of the name, without going through the many modes of such subjectivity. Instead, he contends that "the superiority of the mere _cognition_ of a beautiful object, when that object happened to exist, over the same cognition when the object did not exist, would...be as great as that of the _knowledge_ of a beautiful object over the mere imagination of it" [PE 196-197, M.s italics]. Even if the first statement is true, the second may not be. In what way is Van Gogh's "knowledge" of one of his own paintings preferable to (say) his own "imagination" of it, painting it before or afterwards? This parallels St. Anselm's claim [_Proslogion_, Chapter II] that God as existing outside the intellect is more perfect than as merely existing inside it. Even if the ontological argument is valid, it does not follow that a hundred real Van Goghs are more valuable than a hundred possible ones-the real works are just easily accessible to more minds. In truth the value of what was in Van Gogh's mind's eye is neither identical nor even comparable to the values, the cherished experiences, his paintings created for others. There is no substitute, either for the original or for the originator.

Moore's account maintains that knowledge is a factor indispensable to aesthetically fulfilling experience. It isn't enough to have the right feeling toward the right object; one must have it for the right reasons, and in the right way (notably reminiscent of Aristotle's criteria for exemplifying practical wisdom). In listening to a piece of music, it isn't enough to hear it, to know what composition you are hearing or even to be delighted by it. Your emotion is worthless if it is "unaccompanied by any consciousness" of the musical relationships that make the work successful [PE 192]. If you are not trained to appreciate the work, then your appreciation, if any, is a negligible form of awareness. This isn't snobbery, but a corollary of criteria (i)-(vi). It is also common sense. It applies to participation in crafts, athletics, parliamentary debate, and dozens of other activities not usually associated with (fine) art or the contemplation of nature. Moore is therefore entirely justified in holding that knowledge is an indispensable ingredient in aesthetic experience. While in everyday life and (for the most part) in science, knowledge is a means, giving us "extrinsic advantage", in the aesthetic arena it is "intrinsically superior" to what life (or those situations) would be like in its absence [PE 196]. Moore doesn't say whether these appraisals are the result of performing a series of ITs, comparing the world with knowledge to the world without it. I suspect that one might reach the same conclusions in a variety of ways. However, disagreeing with Moore, expressing skepticism concerning the legitimacy of one or more of the stipulated criteria for aesthetic experience, might compel him to demonstrate (the cogency of) the IT, so as to resolve disputes concerning (meta)standards of taste.

I am happy to come to Moore's defense concerning the role of knowledge in aesthetic contexts. Its meaning is quite simple: objects without perceivers are empty, perceivers without objects are blind. Perhaps a tree does make a sound when it falls in the forest, even if no one is around to hear it. But the value of the sound is minuscule, all by itself. Paintings, poems and symphonies were meant to be seen, read and heard, not to blush unperceived. Both a right-minded subject and a well-constructed object are necessary for aesthetic experience to take place; either one apart from the other is like Aristophanes' lovers in search of their mates. The POU demands as much. Hence, the current discussion fits in with Moore's most extended argument in PE. There is only one problem: if Moore is right, f/v sundering is immediately abolished.

Round 5: What Hath Moore Wrought?

When Moore differentiates between errors of judgment and those of taste, he innocently maintains that this reflects the distinction between fact and value [PE 193]. My judgment that I am viewing the Mona Lisa, when actually sighting a beer can, concerns matters of fact. My judgment that the beer can is prettier than Mona is a value-judgment. Both are wrong, but in different ways. Nothing objectionable (or new) here, although it does prove that the f/v gap receives explicit and favorable attention from Moore [Rohatyn (1982), 182n20], and is not foisted on the text, just to advance (or retard) some pet scholarly thesis extraneous to Moore's own announced purposes.

But what about my knowledge that the Mona Lisa (whether I am seeing it now or not) is a great work of art? If this deserves to be called knowledge, then it follows that "M.L. is a great work" is true. This is not a hypothetical description of an ideal observer's or connoisseur's belief. It does not allude to historical impact or importance (as in "Caesar was a great man"). It is not an oblique depiction of the status of a cultural artifact. It is a value-judgment. It is also, simultaneously, a statement of alleged fact--no more, and no less, an act of interpretation than e.g., the law of gravity or the contention that the earth orbits the sun. One can admit the distinctiveness of terms such as 'good,' 'right,' 'ought,' and their aesthetic counterparts, without being committed to an exclusive segregation of verbal categories, such as the "G-words" and "pro-attitudes" coined by Nowell-Smith. Value-vocabulary indicates conditions to be applied or realized in experience, as by Dewey. Even Moore admits that "an ethical law has the nature not of a scientific law but of a scientific prediction" [PE 155, M.s italics], though this is tinged with disdain for empirical, and therefore merely probable, hypotheses. In any case, the specific aesthetic judgment states a fact because it is true; the corresponding denial is false. Thus, there is no way out. This is all we need to counter-example the f/v dichotomy. We can construct propositions which belong to both categories simultaneously.

Moreover, the knowledge that the M.L. is a great work enhances (increases) the value of an aesthetic encounter, in accordance with what the POU stresses. Thus, a "state of things" [PE 196] exerts (causal) influence over the value of some whole to which it belongs. We must beware of overestimating the value of knowledge, all by itself. Yet directly or indirectly, it changes the outcome, not just of a value appraisal but of value experience. Even mere true beliefs can have this effect: "...a true belief in the reality of an object greatly increases the value of many valuable wholes" [PE 198-199]. How could any of this be, if (as in Hare) values always 'supervene' on facts, or if any of the objections raised on pp. 4-10 were valid? Here it is not a question of the statement of belief or of knowledge, but of the occurrence which the statement reflects. Once again, we have counter-exampled the f/v dichotomy. Anyone who alleges that "...it is not only true that one cannot get an Ought from as Is, it is also significantly true" [Holmes (1981), 405] must first explain how it is possible to segregate moral from "exclusively nonmoral" premises [Ibid., 396]. Otherwise, "deriving" the conclusion that one cannot derive an ought from an is, is both trivial and fallacious.

What about the tree that thuds in the forest without being heard? Does it still exist? Of course. We are not forced to become Idealists. By 1912, Moore "...no longer...held that value could belong to unperceived objects..." [Duncan-Jones (1957), repr. in Ambrose and Lazerowitz (1970), 319]. Only facts preserve their independence in this way. But nine years earlier, Moore already makes bold conjectures whose effect is to undermine the f/v dichotomy, even if he remains blithely unaware of what they entail. On pain of contradiction, Moore is obliged to surrender the thesis formulated on his behalf to rebut Hartman (pp. 51-52). Ontology is no longer irrelevant to value. (We argued for the converse proposition at the outset, but now witness Moore's inner turmoil.

If ontology is relevant to value, then the f/v disjunction is dead. Since the OQA ruled ontology out, the OQA must be ruled out, instead. This does not tell us which ontology is true, or which value-theory to adopt; it merely excludes certain self-refuting extremes. Its poignant effect on Moore is that he must give up, either the OQA or else the insights fought for in PE Chap. VI. His next moves will make this choice even more difficult. Yet Moore never notices just how severely he undermines himself; all in a chapter which lays such heavy emphasis on the value of self-awareness! Ironically, Moore's greatest weakness is also one of his major strengths.

<u>Round 6</u>:   <u>A Thing of Beauty is a Thing Forever</u>

Previous philosophers in search of the highest good have exaggerated the spiritual at the expense of the mundane. They have supposed that the mental life is the exclusive repository of value, and that the material world is either non-contributory or a source of positive evil [PE 205-206]. In tackling this problem, Moore is eventually led to ponder theodicies. In a perfect world, there should be no villains. How then could we enjoy Shakespearean tragedy? Very simply. The stage sufferings would be "purely imaginary" [PE 219], rather than based on antecedently real events, or parallels with life as it is lived. This must be what heaven--or utopia--is like. No one dies, no one is emotionally hurt, no one starves, loses a career, a reputation or a lover. Everything is play. Moore doesn't stop to ask how Shakespeare would get material for his plots, or what emotions the audience might experience if pity and terror were released while watching the play, but enjoined no corresponding moral outside the theatre. "There but for the grace of God go I" is a form of catharsis unavailable in paradise. Somehow perfection must take care of these contingencies, or else secure a trade-off, relinquishing (some) earthly experience to gain uninterrupted tranquility.

Shortly we will see what Moore thinks of all this. Right now his point is that knowledge of the reality of suffering cannot compensate for the pain; it "...will add no positive value to that good great enough to counterbalance such a loss" [PE 219]. Hence, the tapestry theory of evil--evil exists that good may come--is a sophistry. In the best of all possible worlds, evil would be non-existent, or merely a form of play (like the "rest and recreation" planet depicted on an episode of the television series <u>Star Trek</u>, in which the protagonists' inner fantasies were projected in space and time, but could not ultimately harm either the crew of the space ship or any interlopers). "There is no reason to think that any actual evil whatsoever would be contained in the Ideal" [PE 220]. When evil is real, the "total sum of value" is always reduced to a "negative quantity" [PE 220], and things are never positive on balance. "Accordingly, we have no reason to maintain the paradox that an ideal world would be one in which vice and suffering must exist in order that it may contain the goods consisting in the appropriate emotion toward them" [PE 220]. Moore isn't being gloomy; he is simply putting the burden of proof squarely where it belongs: if God exists, there must be a better way in which God could arrange existence. Of course, Moore's refutation of the strong thesis that evil "must" exist leaves a rational believer free to maintain the weaker thesis that a minimum number of 'terps' is logically compatible with the goodness of an omniscient, omnipotent, benevolent Being. But if so, then this Being must perform ITs in which (on at least one occasion) such terps are tolerated as unavoidable components of some particular good. Such a good would not be unmixed, and therefore not Ideal. Hence, we can surpass the impoverished imagination of such a Being, which casts doubt on its alleged perfection.

None of this is meant to deny that, as things stand, it is better (if not intrinsically, then in practical terms) for us to know that evil is real, than to remain ignorant of it. Nor is Moore denying that evil brings out qualities of compassion, courage and heroism which might otherwise be dormant. Covering every base, Moore adds that it is preferable to direct one's compassion toward those who are actually suffering than toward merely imaginary characters, and that it is better to dwell knowingly on "pure fiction" than to entertain false beliefs about the world as it is [PE 219]. None of which negates the claim that in the best of all PWs, evil and ugliness do not exist. The tautologous assertion that they would be bad if they did exist, proves it. Therefore, only in certain cases of "mixed goods" in our world can knowing evil become an asset [PE 220], at least in principle.

This leads Moore to apply the IT to the question of what is evil [PE 208]. Here he urges that the "intrinsic odiousness" of cruelty "...is equally great, whether the pain contemplated really exists or is purely imaginary" [PE 210]. A hundred real lashes are no differernt from a hundred possible ones, though one must also distinguish between pain and cognition of pain, as Wittgenstein and Dennett do. Neither knowledge nor true belief in "...the existence of their objects makes any difference in the degree of their positive demerits" [PE 210, M.s italics], whereas, in considering "worthy affection for a real person," we are justified in weighing "...the additional good consisting in the existence of that person" [PE 210, M.s italics]. Moore is careful to add that belief in the existence of evil is useful as a means, if not as an end; he is not about to advocate self-delusion, on any front. Whether Moore is right or wrong about the details into which he enters is less important than his emphasis on the need to look at, rather than prejudge, specific cases. Moore wants to avoid hasty generalizations, and to prevent us from regarding evils simplistically, as the diametric opposite of goods. How else could things which are "good on the whole" [PE 220, orig. in ital.; also PE 214] ever be understood, unless in a way which avoids black-white fallacies? Above all, it is remarkable that Moore devotes as much space as he does to this topic. With the exception of Rosenkrantz, whose treatise on ugliness is still untranslated, I cannot think of any philosopher who has taken the pains to explore negative values in any detail. Innumerable Christian theologians have discussed evil, but usually indirectly, in light of their adherence to a "privation" theory that (at least nominally) forced them to treat evil as "non-being." This runs afoul of the POU, which admonishes us not to look at good and evil as straightforwardly opposed (although 'good' and 'bad' alike qualify as "simple," at PE 5). Bentham's felicific calculus, despite its crude parody of scientific measurement of experience, not only ranks pains and pleasures, but encourages estimates of subtle in between shades Classical utilitarianism undoubtedly anticipated Moore , even prior to Mill's insistence on 'quality/quantity' nuance. Yet Moore's expansion of that theme deserves credit, too.

Since value is neither exclusively mental nor exclusively physical, it follows that it is to some degree both. The "organic unity" between these categories entails that "...part of what is included in this whole is a cognition of material qualities, and particularly of a vast variety of what are called secondary qualities" [PE 206, M.s italics]. (This is where Hartman may have gotten the inspiration to posit 'tertiary qualities'.) Not just the cognition, but the qualities themselves, count toward overall worth: "...we know that material qualities, even though they be perfectly worthless in themselves, are yet essential constituents of what is far from worthless. What we know to be valuable is the apprehension of just these qualities..." [PE 206, M.s italics]. The chemicals in my body are worth less than $1, but I am beyond price, and my body is not for sale. The pigment and canvas used by Turner in painting a landscape command little on the open market; as transformed by Turner's expert hand, their value grows to several million dollars. Here is a labor theory of value, par excellence!

Irritatingly, Moore oscillates between emphasizing the "cognition" or "apprehension" of the qualities and the qualities themselves. Which is it that he considers valuable, and in relation to what? This problem arises because he already identified "certain states of consciousness" [PE 188] as being the MVPs of life. Now it appears that he is qualifying that thesis, only to reaffirm it immediately. Since nothing short of an object-subject coupling qualifies as an organic unity, there are two ways to reconcile these conflicting comments. One is, to throw out (or modify) the statements which stress subjective awareness alone. The other is, to reinterpret 'object' as nothing but the intentional state which a subject experiences, rather than as something "external" to the experiencer. The first method cleans up Moore's linguistic act, but risks imposing a meaning, albeit a clear and consistent one, on the text. The second method aligns Moore (see p. 33) with the phenomenological tradition, but threatens to compromise his vaunted realism. In consequence, I favor the first approach, but fortunately, it isn't necessary to decide this issue. Even if 'object' is construed in Husserlian fashion, the organic unity still has two poles, separable for purposes of analysis though connected, like form and matter, in experience itself. (Incidentally, this might enhance studies of Moore's "sense-data" theory.) And we can continue to speak (provisionally) of subject and object, provided we don't reify either term.

Regardless of which interpretation we adopt, the outcome of Moore's analysis of the relative value of material vs. mental qualities is the same. Can there be a better world than this one? In principle, yes: "it is just possible that the Absolute Good may be entirely composed of qualities which we cannot even imagine" [PE 184, M.s capitals], and therefore that it is beyond our powers to "discover what the Ideal is" [PE 184-185]. But--speaking of trade-offs--in a world devoid of matter, devoid of bodies, we should have to give up all of the goods that we know, for things about which we can at most speculate. There is no evidence that such a world (as opposed to a future improvement of our own) would indeed be better. Until this burden of proof is met

> XVII....we are entitled to assert that material qualities are a necessary constituent of the Ideal; that, though something utterly unknown might be better than any world containing either them or any other good we know, yet we have no reason to suppose that anything whatever would be better than a state of things in which they would be included. To deny and exclude matter, is to deny and exclude the

best we know [PE 207, M.'s italics and capitals].

To me, this is the most stirring passage in PE. I can only dimly evoke a sense of the liberating impact it must have had on Moore's guilt-ridden Victorian contemporaries. In 1899, Moore disapproved of masturbation "as an end" [Levy (1979), 207], but, as Russell alone saw, the real intent was to deny that life consisted of "isolated passionate moments" punctuated by drear [Levy (1979), 237-238]. Moore may owe something to the advent of Freud (The Interpretation of Dreams was first published in 1900). But his true predecessors are Aristotle and J.S. Mill, insofar as an emphasis on life as a continuous process, and on value as an overall quality of experience are concerned. This is consistent with, and well-articulated by, the POU. Yet, Moore's life-affirming instincts do cause trouble for his official views on value. If matter is "the best we know" then (e.g.) beautiful objects are valuable (in part) because of their objecthood. The (referents of) facts themselves are good; the f/v dichotomy explodes. It makes no difference whether matter is stuff, or only a set of intentional states. For the latter comprise facts, too. Indeed, "counterfactuals" are unintelligible unless we can compare or check them against established facts, especially when making disciplined conjectures about how history might (not) have been different [Elster (1978), 192-218]. Hence, "possible worlds" exist along a continuum, not in separate realms. (Otherwise there would be no (logical) truths valid in all possible worlds, except by coincidence. But chance entails at least one world devoid of such truths. Hence, a fortuitous conjunction of "transworld" (necessary) truths is internally inconsistent.)

Since Moore tells us not to exaggerate the importance of mental as opposed to physical qualities, I am inclined to take him at his word, rather than to advocate a sophisticated reinterpretation of 'physical' along post-Berkeleyan lines. But even such reduction of the physical to the realm of the mental (taking care to redraw all the appropriate contrasts within the phenomenal field) closes the f/v gap, as soon as value is attributed to the states of mind (or body) themselves. And the linguistic domain suffers the same fate, since propositions about value take their cues from whatever situation Moore acknowledges. If "facts themselves" have value, then we cannot be coy about admitting it. Of course, we can draw verbal distinctions without ontological counterparts; but they serve no purpose, except to promote self-delusion.

The dilemma now facing Moore was already on the horizon on page 65, when we alluded to an additional problem confronting (the Intuition of) PWs. For if one of those PWs is ours, then facts must intrude on our value-judgments. And how could it be otherwise, since even an array of conditions a-n which (by design) is entirely fictitious is still the invention of someone situated in an actual, not just a possible, world. (This upholds Aristotle's insistence that actuality is logically prior to possibility.) Moreover, the conception of a completely empty universe is self-referentially impossible, since an agent must conceive of it. Granted, we can posit universe A while standing outside it, in universe B. But an "empty universe" is a contradiction in terms, since if it were empty it wouldn't be a universe! If it contains nothing else, it contains the thought that it contains nothing else. Hence the IT vindicates Descartes' <u>cogito</u> and all of its philosophical brethren. Berkeley was right: someone is always about in the Quad. So was Parmenides, in denying that one could meaningfully say that non-Being was not. No matter whether we contemplate the best, worse, largest or sparsest of all PWs, the self-transcendence of the symbol users who make and reflect on their comparisons insures that fact cannot be divorced from value, be it on the linguistic or the ontological plane ([Habermas (1971), 138-139 and Gewirth (1978), 64] use a similar argument to ground equality as a precondition for dialogue and action, respectively.)

Significantly, at PE 207, Moore does not flinch from drawing conclusions which necessarily yield the consequences just stated. While there is no precedent for such radicalism on his part, the rigor of his partial analysis makes the inferences which follow from it as ineluctable as their ensuing clash with PE Chap. I principles. It would be a miscalculation to regard the IT procedure as an idiosyncracy, elimination of which saves Moore from further embarrassment or difficulty. The assumptions Moore makes, when followed through, are germane to any worthwhile account of PWs. The meaning of modality, not the waywardness of Moore's posits, dictates the results. So do the conditions for pondering the exercise of modality: the presence of reflexive intelligence. The f/v gap is sewn up on all sides: ontological, logical, linguistic, and epistemic.

What is remarkable is that Moore could be so oblivious to the manner in which his Chapter VI insights go contrary to everything he established in Chapter I. Is this the product of a sublimated yet renegade Hegelian id, running counter to the censoring tendencies of an analytic super-ego? Is Moore's failure to perceive what he is doing a case of intellectual repression, allowing him to maintain ego-control? Conversely, is the unconscious another name for the ideal worlds we create in our dreams, invented precisely because reality (society) denies us the opportunity to do so overtly? We should not be surprised if Bloomsburyites found Moore's restrained fantasies an attractive counterpoint to Freud's unmasking of self-deception. Nor is it a coincidence that psychoanalysis and linguistic analysis arose at about the same time. Both involve the search for essences; one declares that rationalizations are hopeless, the other, that the search for them is.

Moore would quickly remind us that he never intended to sabotage ethics, and that PE Chaps. I-V demolitions were a necessary preparation, or rubbish-clearing, for the Chapter VI dénouement which was planned all along. There is much merit to this proposal. Of course, Moore consistently holds that 'good' is meaningful, and his "non-naturalism" does not commit him to Platonism, either at the beginning or (as should be obvious) at the end of PE. But how can we square the OQA with the arguments which climax at PE 207? To accept Moore's Ideal is to deny that value-debate is in principle endless (unless we sanitize the OQA by turning it into a congenial avowal of fallibility). Quite apart from the struggle over the f/v dichotomy, it follows that PE Chap. VI shouldn't even have been written, if we go by the standard created by the five chapters which precede it. Unless my reading of Moore is totally perverse, he has produced two mutually incompatible world-views. They are not kept segregated, in air-tight logical compartments, since the POU figures prominently in both of them. Yet, they do not interpenetrate; Moore shows no signs that anything is amiss. This was a blessing; had Moore been aware of what he was up to, he might have stopped short of producing either the OQA or the heroic insights of Chapter VI. Since the former is self-defeating, there is no need to seek for a reconciliation (which does not entail that Chapter VI is entirely cogent, or beyond criticism). In 1903, while struggling to formulate this novel conception, Moore might not have seen how to pass beyond or synthesize ideas. Hence, we should be grateful to Moore, regardless whether it was daring, silliness or neurotically conditioned blindness that prompted him to manufacture the several forms of doublethink which he bequeathed to us. Annoying? Yes, but also rewarding--which proves Moore's point about the role of mixed goods, in an unremittingly imperfect world. The Bacchanalian revel is uninterrupted; the temporal return is eternal.

CHAPTER VIII

THE AUTOPSY OF FACT/VALUE

A. Tidying Up

1. The fact/value dichotomy is dead. Moore helps kill it for us, apart from the arguments already brought against it on pages 1-10. His arguments are fascinating in their own right, and are not duplicated anywhere else in the literature. This alone repays the work of intense scrutiny, though it magnifies the difficulties of interpreting PE.

2. Jubilation over the demise of the f/v dichotomy does not imply that we should exult at Moore's expense. (To forestall premature bragging, we will revive the f/v disjunction in Chapter X, pp. 115-119.) PE may be self-contradictory, but this is true of many great works in philosophy. Logical impasses are to be expected. Provided that inconsistency is not treated as symptomatic of a thinker's downfall, such exercises in textual scholarship are not an antiquarian irrelevancy; the ad hominem circumstantial is unjustly maligned, and has a legitimate dialectical role to play [Johnstone (1959), 129, 131]. Besides, I admire Moore for his ability to break through orthodoxy, in defiance of self-imposed, no less than of socially transmitted, categories and principles. This deserves the highest commendation, disregarding the sporadic and submerged character of his revolt. Few of us do better in life. Besides, it has taken 80 years to discover the unofficial Moore. Why so long? Are we captives of the cultural mind-set from which he managed at times to break free? Is the founder or chief proponent of a doctrine less locked in, less gripped by it than his followers and successors? While hindsight may exceed Moore's capacity for self-insight, what if someday a similar humbling critique awaits ourselves?

3. It's easy to become indignant about "...how little subsequent attention has been paid to it [PE Chap. VI] by professional ethicists themselves. It is as if Principia Ethica had only five chapters and the last had never been written" [Levi (1974), 282]. Indeed, for the better part of this century, PE had only one chapter, and the last five were never written. It seems only just to restore the organic

unity of Moore's own text. But ancestral piety isn't
satisfying if it pays no other dividends. Hence,
it's not enough to lament that "Moore's ideas on
value deserve more attention. He brought
contemplation of goodness and beauty back into the
centre of the moral scene, where they had not stood
since Plato. He balanced the busy over-emphasis on
activity of the Protestant West by sounding a trumpet
for the inner life" [Midgley (1981), 62]. Perhaps,
though Moore might not recognize himself in this
description. Did Moore's concentration upon "the
inner life" favor or create waves of narcissism? Did
Moore rashly forget all about "...the joy of
communion...the joy of active leadership in a great
moral cause...the joy of difficult problem-solving
and intellectual contemplation..." [Levi (1974),
284)? Some artists still find Moore's ideas
inspiring; he does not lack for latter-day champions
[Murdoch (1971), 4]. But do his supporters and
adherents really know Moore, or have they
romanticized him? Would they still admire him if
they detected the inconsistency, the implicit
<u>reductio</u> of non-naturalism, at the heart of PE? Is
part of their admiration based on the 'art for art's
sake' paradigm, which so easily turns into a
stereotype? These fears are compounded by a
retrospective assessment of Moore's thoughts: if
matter is the best we know, doesn't this rout the
pretension to foster or lead "the inner life"? Maybe
not. 'Matter' as Moore uses it is ambiguous--perhaps
fatally so, despite our sustained effort (pp. 77-80)
to smooth it over. If material qualities are really
a species of the mental, then Midgley is upheld, and
admiration for Moore's defense of the MVPs does not
degenerate into idolatry. However, this doesn't
settle things. Consider the meaning of the slogan
'objects without perceivers are empty, perceivers
without objects are blind' (above, p. 72). Applied
to value, this still entails means positing inter-
subjective entities of experience. Picasso and
Stravinsky exist for all of us. Our "subjective"
contributions to various organic wholes nuance them
in different ways, but this does not prevent us from
communicating about the elements that they have in
common. An inner life is also, perforce, an outer
life. Participation in art and nature can get along
with nothing less. Emphasis on the "inner life" is a
metaphor which expresses some degree of different-
ness, of individual worth or uniqueness.

Am I being purely verbal and picky? I insist on making the point, nonetheless. Moore does say that "certain states of consciousness" [PE 188] are the highest goods, and so we are obliged to crack an old chestnut. This is felicitously read as an abbreviated allusion to a transaction in which both consciousness and its object(s) play an essential role in the determination of value--for otherwise, Moore is in imminent danger of violating the POU, and of falling into the very errors ridiculed (with Plato's help) in his critique of hedonism, in PE Chap. III. Even once we redefine 'object(s)' as Berkeleyan percepts (Moorean sense-data?), we are still compelled to acknowledge the value of the once external, now internalized world, whose constituents differ from themselves and from (each of) us.

The foregoing account is familiar and repetitious, but necessary, thanks to Moore's persistent tendency to lapse into mentalist habits [cf. pp. 25, 28]. Consider the definition of beauty again: "...that of which the admiring contemplation is good in itself" [PE 201, 208]. When we first looked at this (p. 67), we were so preoccupied with the NF, we failed to notice that the definition is quite ambiguous. Is the admiring contemplation the (sole) good here? Is "that of which" it is the admiring contemplation the good? Or is the good a combination of both? To avoid jeopardizing the POU, I prefer the last possibility. Since Moore objects to definitions which are predicated on mere feeling (such as the Thomistic formula, 'the beautiful is that which when seen pleases us'), he has no right to complain if a critic should find his definition unconvincing, for exactly the same reason. Or is "admiring contemplation" a bloodless, emotionless thought? If so, then Moore is not worth saving; Midgley can have him. Moore's insistence on the unity of belief and feeling, both in aesthetic enjoyment and in conducting appraisals [PE 193-194; above, p. 70] overcomes the threat of psychological primitivity. But his various stabs at giving definitions make a more compelling case for the indefinability of concepts than any of Moore's official criticisms of definition as inherently circular.

4. The preceding remarks may justify my apparent harshness towards Moore's few current sympathizers. I cannot be their instant ally, at least not when it comes to PE. Too many authors have

caricatured Moore, even when they thought they were
praising him. Platonist, non-naturalist, promoter of
aesthetic ideality, and--not least--repudiator of any
logical connection between fact and value. Those who
bought shares in Moore's stock understood PE Chap. I
only too well. In their visceral response to Chapter
VI, did they stop to read the fine print, or only
glance at the contract prior to signing it? Both
ends of PE have been misunderstood in different ways,
by groups with different (and sometimes overlapping)
interests. I hope my scruples regarding Moore's
backers are not mistaken for scholarly
possessiveness. No one can be sure of their own
motives, and I cannot rule out the possibility that I
suffer from silly jealousy over the "rights" to
transmit a dead man's legacy. Spleen notwithstanding, the main question is whether Moore has
suffered unjustly from acquiring the wrong
reputation. He can never be a forthright, thorough
naturalist such as Aristotle or Mill, Dewey or Perry.
But his ambivalence does qualify him, at least in my
estimate, as a "reluctant" naturalist, that is,
someone who cannot follow through on his
conceptual inclinations, because they are too
conflicting or else too heretical to take root. At
the same time, his instincts are too powerful for him
to ignore. Hence he fudges, compromises, and
conceals. The psycho-drama which unfolds on the
pages of PE shouts for attention. Yet, Moore's
unorthodoxy was never revealed, either to himself or
by others. This takes place only under the pressure
of confronting Chapter I with Chapter VI, and vice
versa. The internal collapse of Moore's system is
the inevitable consequence of blunting the OQA razor
by scratching the Ideal diamond.

B. Pluralism and Its Problems

1. What is the meaning of life? Permit me to
answer on Moore's behalf. There are lots of people.
Some of them are quite nice, and supremely worth
getting to know. There are also many things in this
world [O'Connor (1982), 2 provides a categorical
inventory], waiting to be encountered. Some of these
are quite wonderful, and you must exert yourself, to
come in contact with and enjoy them. Goods as well
as evils exist in profuse abundance--as well as many
phenomena that are intermediate (indifferent). The
good life means more than having a surplus of good
times, memorable or even "consummatory" experiences.

It means having a life plan, a goal, from which contentment emerges as a by-product [see Elster (1983) for a detailed and ingenious study of this phenomenon]. As Mill justly observed, "...the conscious ability to do without happiness gives the best prospect of reaching such happiness as is attainable" [Utilitarianism, Chapter II, para. 16]. Satisfaction is not an aim but an outcome. We must dig deep inside, determine who we are and what we want from life, and then strive to achieve it. Moore doesn't comment on whether the process of struggling to reach one's goals is as valuable as their achievement. But he would undoubtedly say that denial of opportunity is more of a tragedy than mere failure. Whatever the life pattern, it has (in principle) its own organic unity, and we inspect and approve of it, on (isolation-style) reflection. There may be as many plans as there are individuals striving to fulfill them; the elements of the good life just proposed are what they all have in common. This is what makes casuistry, or the study of particular cases, so difficult; for it combines the most abstract with the most concrete aspects of valuation. It is at once "...the goal of ethical investigation" [PE 5] and the last thing many philosophers are prepared to discuss. There is only the consolation that the formal constituents of the good life are universal, interchangeable. To a limited extent, this licenses the claim that passing judgments is impersonal--I can judge the fitness of your life-configuration and you can judge mine, though we remain ignorant about respective intimacies, perforce, cannot substitute for (i.e., live) each other's lives.

One remark about the timelessness of the criteria is in order. For Moore, past and future make no difference to the status of value judgments. Grant that a life is found good in the living of it (C.I. Lewis), but then it must be such both before and after living it, for any (thought) experimenter who dares it. Goodness now, goodness tomorrow and goodness yesterday are all the same, by the identity of value indiscernibles [Chapter IX, below, pp. 95, 100-102]. Of course, through ignorance or delay, we may allow opportunities for self-realization to pass us by, or else, we may grow and take advantage of them before it is too late; but this feature of time influences action, not truth. Likewise, the universe may change in ways that preclude or enable value to come into being. This does not affect the correctness of hypothetical 'if...then' propositions which state the relation between goodness and the appropriate circumstances for it.

As Moore's examples (enjoying King Lear vs. indiscriminately smashing some crockery [E 102]) suggest, pleasures are not to be weighed or placed on a Benthamic utility interval scale. Even though promoting a balance of pleasure over pain is obviously desirable [E 8-11], pleasure taken as a "correct criterion" of right and wrong "...is impossible to prove" [E 101; M.s italics in both quotes]. Moore doesn't mention the NF in this connection; rather, his argument is that the pleasure-standard assumes a logically prior conception of intrinsic value [E 102]. Moore's natural ally here is J.S. Mill, yet Moore inveighs against Mill's distinction between quantity and quality of pleasure [PE 77-81], arguing that any "judgment of preference" likewise presupposes an Intuition, i.e., "...a judgment utterly independent of all considerations as to whether one thing is more desired or pleasanter than another" [PE 79]. This, he insists, clinches the case for the indefinability of 'good' [PE 79]. Even if it does not, Moore still contends that a quantitative approach to pleasure reduces itself to absurdity [E 102]. Together with the factors mentioned above that belong to (the conception of) the good life, this makes Moore far more of an adherent to Mill's humanistic vision than he cares to admit, or than his misdirected critique [PE 64-74] of Mill's supposed bungling of the proof of utility [cf. Rohatyn (1976), Chapter III] might lead one to suspect.

Our conclusion is that Moore is an unabashed pluralist. Not only is there "no single criterion of beauty" [PE 202], which we should expect as a corollary of the POU, but also, quite concretely, the more beautiful things and people there are, the merrier: "...that two such admirable persons should exist is greatly better than that there should be only one..." [PE 196]. Diversity is a higher good than monotony (as performing an IT discloses). Fortunately, diversity is also real. For once, the world is as it ought to be.

2. Once we ponder the implications of value-plenitude, the situation quickly grows complicated. Is plenitude in efffect all the way to infinity, or until we reach an asymptotic figure? Moore doesn't

say. Over-population does not enter into his
thinking, and why should it? Values aren't facts,
they are intangibles; they don't take up space or
compete for resources. Besides, even if they did,
mere facts qua facts cannot become objects of
aesthetic rapture or even of balanced, yet emotionally committed, IT contemplation. And, as PE Chap. V
alleges, facts are always too variable to yield
genuine knowledge. The result is a mutually
problematic set of propositions:

    i.   There is no knowledge of fact.

    ii. There is knowledge of value.

    iii. The existence of certain objects and experiences is valuable.

    iv. Knowledge that certain objects (exist and) are valuable, increases the value of the complex wholes in which such knowledge figures.

    If (i) is true, then (ii) cannot be, since (iii)
alleges a fact. If (iii) is false, or else
meaningless, then (iv) cannot be true, because (iv)
is parasitic on the truth of (iii). If neither (iii)
nor (iv) is true (either false or meaningless,
respectively), then (ii) is false. If (ii) is false,
then we are thrown back upon the f/v dichotomy, with
a vengeance. Moore can't have (iii) and (iv) without
the denial of (i); and he can't have (i) without the
denial of (ii). Not only does this force him (or us)
to choose between Chapters I and VI, but it ends up
PE denying both (the knowledge of) facts and (the
objectivity of) values, which is more than any tough-
minded skeptic (including Hume) ever did. If there
is no knowledge of fact, then there can be no
knowledge of value, either (for discussion, see pp.
91-92). This is why the truth of (i) entails the
falsity (or denial) of (ii) (for a proof of the
converse proposition, see p. 92 below).

    Of course, 'knowledge' has many meanings, and if
we equivocate, there is no problem about reconciling
(i)-(iv). This I refuse to do. Even providing
subscripts does not rid us of handicaps, since some
senses of that term are bound to be more honorific
than others. Hence, this tactic merely evades and
shifts the problem, without solving it. Whatever
'knowledge' may mean: justified true belief,

warranted assertability, corroborable or falsifiable hypotheses or conjecture, acquaintance, or know-how, must be kept consistent. However, this does not affect any substantive point.

It is not astonishing that in the decades after 1903, especially during the heyday of positivism, Moore's readers had but little incentive to peek beyond PE 21. Those who did, made no startling discoveries; even Chapters V-VI do much to reinforce one's conviction that trying to make value-theory viable is futile. But those who persevered or who found the final episode aristocratic and enchanting, were seduced either by Moore's rhetoric (hard to believe) or else by their own expectations and hopes. They should have been wary and bothered by what they read there rather than enthralled. This is why I mistrust reactions to Chapter VI which applaud the "nobility" of its outlook, without examining whether it has any foundation. Only a prisoner of the 'two cultures' syndrome could bask in the cold sunshine of Moore's denudation of fact and of value [Olthius (1968), 161-162] without freezing, or seeking refuge elsewhere. It is to Moore's credit that he does not merely acquiesce in the not so inexorable logic of his opening gambits, but gradually rejects or implicitly overthrows them.

For, if (i) is true and (ii) is false, or vice versa, or even if we regard both (i) and (ii) as mistaken, it is still possible to rescue Moore from oblivion. Whoever affirms (i), (ii) or their denials is committed to (v) the distinction between truth and falsity, and hence to the virtue of maintaining that distinction. One who considers (e.g.) (iii) and (iv) to be meaningless is likewise committed, if not to the truth then to the "heuristic value" of such conjectures. (Recall our examination (pp. 10, 46) of intellectual integrity as an inadvertent value thesis.) Hence, propositions likewise presuppose values, as C.S. Peirce emphasized in labeling logic a "normative science" [Peirce, Collected Papers 1.573. Also see 1.611, 2.82, 4.240, 5.111, 5.533. At 5.35, Peirce describes logic as "the doctrine of what we ought to think," perforce "an application of the doctrine of what we deliberately choose to do, which is Ethics." Midway through 2.198, Peirce avers that "life can have but one end. It is Ethics which defines that end. It is, therefore, impossible to be thoroughly and rationally logical except upon an ethical basis." [For further commentary, cf. Apel

(1980), 257, 260.] The price to be paid for such a frankly transcendental argument is the dissolution of the OQA [pp. 45-47]. We are more than willing to pay it, since we have come to bury the naturalistic fallacy, not to praise it. Shortly we shall ask whether Moore might be so disposed.

3. The plenitude problem brings forth another, to which it is closely related. In the best of all PWs, goods would never vie with or exclude one another. Moore's strictures on the bankruptcy of theodices (pp. 74-76) trade heavily on this point. But what do we do when we are faced with something less than the best--whether in our imagination, or in a situation that calls for prompt action? Whenever the realization of one set of goods conflicts with or impinges on others that we cherish, Moore must resolve the dispute by appealing strictly to Intuition, and the relative order among goods that Intuition ratifies. All this *is* Platonic, and it justly merits Midgley's curt assessment: "The abstraction which leaves out the actions themselves is crippling" [Midgley (1981), 67]. Herman Kahn, Tom Beauchamp, Herbert Simon, and J.J.C. Smart, all of whom know the mathematical lingo of cost-benefit analysis by heart, are not spared the necessity of falling back on an *a priori* principle or presumption-the decision to apply (and abide by) the cost-benefit standard itself. And how do we validate, if not by appealing to yet more basic principles, culminating in a plea for self-evidence? Intuition gives no protection against the OQA; nothing can (the OQA can't even provide a guarantee against itself!). But since Intuition makes short work of argumentative procedures, it is easy to see why Moore, having ruled out all the remaining options, thought that by passing up ratiocination he had found a loophole through which *his* specific rankings might slip [cf. p. 64].

4. If we nicely grant Moore this one favor, would all remaining doubts about the internal coherence of PE vanish? No, because the NF cautions repeatedly against, and then outlaws, such arbitrariness. We have only to cite versions (10) and (12), or e., f., and g. as a warrant for the arrest of the PE Chap. VI bandits. But the indictment works both ways. If there is knowledge of value (p. 89, prop. (ii) above), then value is a fact, both logically and ontologically--which is why prop. (iii) follows from (ii). If knowledge *has*

value (p. 89, prop. (iv)), then not only is the existence of such knowledge a "valuable fact," but it serves as the prototype for construction of a transcendental argument, whence the logical priority of certain norms over any facts, of conditions for experience over what they make possible. The preceding sentence is suggestively Kantian. One thinks immediately of regulative principles as first cousins of this approach (including Kant's attempt to shield causality from Hume's critique of induction). Would Moore approve of this strategy? We could sell it to his ghost, by conversing with him as follows: (I) It is a logical extension of your remarks at PE 194-207. (II) It does not run afoul of the NF, except for the OQA which, by the same reasoning, runs itself aground. Versions (5) and (6), for example, tell us never to confuse two distinct predicates or objects. Fine; a valuable fact can straddle both categories, extensionally, yet satisfy Moore's Butlerian demand for intensional discreteness and irreducibility. So long as this is not a license for advocating 'supervenience' (below, pp. 97-98, 101; above, pp. 8-9, 40-41), all is well. The minute it feigns to promote the latter, the familiar reductio argument comes into play: value is a fact, facts presuppose values, therefore, unless there is knowledge of (some) value, in principle there is no knowledge of (any) fact. Hence, the truth of prop. (ii) entails the denial of (i); this is the converse of what page 86 established. (III) It is in harmony with your own quest for absolutes, and (IV) It agrees with your own reliance on Kantian terminology [cf. p. 28].

The ghost might respond as follows: I am sorry I caused all this trouble. I really had no suspicion my text was so opaque. I tried to be straightforward; when I wrote PE my purpose was single-minded. I apologize for the misleading manner in which I stated my position; however, I am not responsible for your philosophical mistakes. You continue to write as though the notion of intrinsic value were a mere sidelight, when it is central to everything I have to say. Your claims to triumph over me are premature, since you have shunned that concept from the beginning. If you really want to find out what's what, what I stand for, you must study this topic with immense care. Then we may talk again. P.S. Don't overrate Kant, or my dependence on him. The "Copernican revolution" in epistemology is grounded in the same confusions [PE 133] as the idealisms and a hypothetically pure, supersensible will is just another variant of the linguistic dodge that piety is what is pleasing to the gods [<u>Euthyphro</u> 10A]. Since Kant commits the NF [PE 129], please don't make such Kantisms my verbal model; don't use them to convey my most salient theses.

    The ghost is right. We have deferred examining the meaning of intrinsic value long enough. It's time to give the departed his logical due.

CHAPTER IX

EXORCISING INTRINSIC VALUE

A. The Evidence

(1) In 1903, Moore equates 'this is good' with 'this would be good, if it existed' [PE 123; noted by Duncan-Jones (1957), repr. in Ambrose and Lazerowitz (1970), 307]. Everything he writes on intrinsic value (IV) thereafter is in effect a reformulation of this casual and off-handed statement. As we have remarked, the concept of intrinsic value (IV) is first brought forward in Chapter I [PE 17], but it remains for later publications to attempt a sophisticated elucidation of what PE leaves implicit.

(2) In Ethics, published in 1912, Moore repeats several of PE's major contentions, providing a modest calculus to aid in grasping the POU [E, 103-105] while reemphasizing that value is not a "single kind of thing" [E, 106]. The definition of IV remains at an impasse: "...there is no characteristic whatever which belongs to all things that are intrinsically good and only to them--except simply the one that they all are intrinsically good and ought always to be preferred to nothing at all, if we had to choose between an action whose sole effect would be one of them and one which would have no effects at all" [E, 106; M.s italics]. Despite the initial disclaimer, this passage is interesting insofar as it (tacitly) applies the isolation test (IT) to ward off the possibility that non-being might outrank being on the scale of values. (How could it, since this would eliminate the tester!) So Moore's defense of pluralism acknowledges a lower, if not an upper, bound [compare pp. 88, 91, above]. It also shows that Moore desperately wants to tie the results of ITs to choice, to prospective action, contrary to the fearful tone of PE Chap. V, which would invalidate all lifestyles, except for the conservative, contemplative variety that casual reading of Chapter VI appears to support.

Moreover, the hypothetical conditions under which IV judgments are made confirm the analysis that value is contingent upon variable "circumstances," without in the least compromising the distinction between intrinsic and instrumental goods [Korsgaard (1983), 192]. Without oxygen, or carbon dioxide, life disappears; yet the value of life is not (directly) proportional to the presence of stable elements in the atmosphere. The continuation of "the particular relations and causal conditions under which we live" [Korsgaard (1983), 185] is indeed a prerequisite for the IV of a painting, poem or symphony, but hardly what makes them esteemable.

(3) In 1922, Moore travels down this very same road. The vexing phrase "depends solely on the intrinsic nature of the thing in question" [CIV, 260, orig. in ital.] itself requires explication, before it can suffice as a definition of 'IV' [see Pastin (1975), 380-381 for a close analysis of Moore's "test for intrinsic value" as independence from means status]. Moore serves us a series of brilliant but trickly clarifications. For something to possess IV:

a.1. "...it is impossible for what is strictly one and the same thing to possess that kind of value at one time, or in one set of circumstances, and not to possess it at another..." [CIV, 260-261, M.s italics].

a.2. Likewise, "...if x and y can have a different intrinsic value, only where their intrinsic natures are different, it follows that one and the same thing must always have the same intrinsic value" [CIV, 261].

b. "A kind of value is intrinsic if an only if, when anything possesses it, that same thing or anything exactly like it would necessarily or must always, under all circumstances, possess it in exactly the same degree" [CIV, 265, M.s italics].

c. "...if A is beautiful and B is not, you could know a priori that A and B are not exactly alike..." [CIV, 271, M.s italics].

Doesn't al. already refute what we just said in (2) above about the variability of (intrinsic) value in light of changing circumstances? Not at all. What Moore is offering here is an idealization, akin to what scientists routinely do in positing frictionless planes, or other logically conceivable but empirically unrealizable states of affairs. Quotes a2., b., c. disclose Moore's intentions, simply by refining the use of the "if...then" locution introduced in 1903. Fortified by this analogy, it follows that no actual thing, event or relation has IV, except approximately. However, there are some very good approximations--again, exactly as in scientific explanation. This also explains Moore's vigorous defense of the slogan 'matter is the best we know,' in PE Chap. VI. Indeed, the definitions listed above are as Leibnizian as can be; this time, Moore's emphasis falls on the identity of value indiscernibles (IVI), which is a (purposely) fictional standpoint, as is surveying an array of possible worlds. Therefore, it legitimates the latter activity.

Moore's definitions connote, but they do not denote. They are general ground rules for conducting ITs, standards by which to guide real-world judgments. They are not (presumably) objects of value themselves. Nor do they guarantee that the real world will fulfill abstract expectations; on the contrary, it is bound to let us down in some respects (theodicies, beware!). Of course, we are free to disagree with Moore's definitions, which shows, not that 'good' is indefinable but that the OQA is alive if not healthy. The resort to Intuition, so prominent in 1903, is a muted presence here, which is just as well in virtue of its illicit character [cf. pp. 64-65]. But why beat Moore with his own stick? We have done enough of that already.

(4) In 1932, Moore concentrates on the phrase "experiences worth having for their own sakes." This strikes me as a new synonym for 'good' or 'IV,' not as indicating any shift in his outlook. Indeed, the POU is nothing if not an axiom about the coupling between experiencer and experienced that is mandatory for experience to be worthwhile. He offers four criteria to elucidate what the new terminology means, to wit:

i. If two different experiences are both worth having for their own sakes, then they must have the same "character."

ii. Equivalence between two experiences is one thing; the experiences themselves are another, and "cannot possibly be identical" with the "character" that equates them.

iii. Two different experiences may have the same "complex of characters" yet differ in value.

iv. We must distinguish between what "...justifies us in saying that an experience is worth having for its own sake" and the given experience. These two are "never identical," since it is always logically possible to have two or more experiences which are equal to each other in value. [All quotes taken from 1932 Aristotelian society symposium on "Is Goodness a Quality?" repr. in PP (1959), at 100, M.s italics].

Point (i) is unproblematic, though it is not as strong as the principle of IVI, iterated 10 years prior. Point (iv) reminds us that there can be more than one instance of the same kind of goodness, also that experience is one thing, its conceptualization another. Point (ii) extends this, to affirm the conceptual autonomy of the notion of identity--a bit of Aristotelian ontology left over, or else revived, from 30 years in the past. Only point (iii) is troublesome. How can two experiences have the same configuration of qualities, yet not be value-identical? Doesn't this outright violate the IVI? And if so, what is Moore saying now? To find out, we must revert to Moore's comments a decade earlier.

B. The Dilemma

Back in the 1922 paper, Moore qualifies his idealizations by remarking that there are predicates "...which do not depend solely on the intrinsic nature of what possesses them," so that "...it is not true that if x possesses them and y does not, x and y must differ in intrinsic nature" [CIV, 271; M.s italics]. This is harmless enough; x and y might differ in inessential respects, in their accidents rather than their defining properties. But then Moore adds something much more devastating:

XVIII....I do not see how it can be deduced from any logical law, that if A is beautiful, anything that were exactly like A would be beautiful too, in exactly the same degree [CIV, 272].

This appears to contradict A (3) def. b, stated just a page earlier in the 1922 essay. However, it does cohere with A (4) pt. (iii). It also raises the strong suspicion that Moore is about to foreshadow supervenience. For what else could the (onto)logical

independence of value from factual identity be based
upon? This impression strengthens, as Moore draws a
subtle distinction between depending upon an
intrinsic nature or property and being one. IV is
"unique" in being only in the former category, not
the latter. It is therefore a "non-intrinsic
property" [CIV, 273], yet it cannot be merely
extrinsic, either. Moore, therefore, confesses
himself unable to identify the "...characteristic
belonging to intrinsic properties which predicates of
value never possesses" [CIV, 274]. This leaves him
exactly where he was in 1912--or 1903. Like Locke's
"I know not what," Moore believes in values as
distinctive entities (and subjects of discourse),
"only I can't see what it is" that makes values what
they are [CIV, 274; M.s italics]. The 1932 paper
softly echoes this cry of helplessness, by assuming
what Moore's 1922 ignorance allegedly proved: that
one can give a "complete description" of any object
without having to "...mention any predicates of value
it possessed" [CIV, 274; M.s italics]. This move is
an afterthought, rather than a concealed premise in
Moore's argument. It is also spurious. The sudden
reinsertion of the f/v dichotomy in this context
opens up a promising (sic) avenue for later debunkers
of the NF, such as John Searle [Rohatyn (1976),
Chapter IV]. But this puts Moore in the same state
as PE Chap. I left his opponents in. By contrast,
Hartman's proposal to construe values as tertiary
qualities, super-super-sets, which is perfectly
consistent with Moore's "...hypostatization of groups
or classes as being among the constituents of the
universe" [O'Connor (1982), 154] looks more
attractive, if not as pure metaphysics then as a
likely explanation for Moore's brave but abject shrug
of nescience [cf. pp. 41-42].

C. The Solution

The easy way out is to say that we have yet
another instance of Moore's craving for antitheses.
This doesn't reconcile Moore with himself, or do
anybody else much good. Nor is Moore's confusion on
this issue merely a (psycho-) logical duplication of
his original ambiguous constructions. By 1922, even
Moore is baffled, whereas in 1903, only the patient,
acute, distanced reader would experience puzzlement.
Moreover, the 1922 inconsistency occurs between one
paragraph and the next, and concerns one proposition
(or definitional clause), reiterated over some ten

pages of closely knit text. Whereas the 1903
exegetical dilemmas rebound from the beginning of PE
to the end, and back again. They muddy and purify
the same waters. They alternatively reinforce and
collapse Moore's largest, most ambitious thought
edifice. The reverberations are deep, the effects of
disaster, quite permanent. PE was meant to move
ethics in a new direction, not to create roadblocks
and obstacles preventing it from ever accomplishing
anything. It has been systematically misread and
misappreciated for three-fourths of a century,
admired for the wrong reasons and cursed by its own
success. While Moore did (as Jerome Schneewind
complains) mischievously unravel many of the complex
knots that Sidgwick had carefully tied, he did not
suffer from the delusion that moral dilemmas were
tidy, or philosophical ones simple to resolve. We
must save Moore both from his reputation and his
influence, which have distorted our perception of his
thought and probably clouded his own. Moore's
modesty and stubborn independence were real enough,
but they were also postures which kept the outside
world at a safe distance. Like Garbo, Moore knew
that the price of fame was loss of soul. So he
cultivated an unassuming naivete which became his
public mask. It made him a minor celebrity, while
protecting him from self-destruction. It was his
image, both concealing and becoming his personality.
Consequently, when we read PE today, we must make a
special effort to recapture the mood and feeling-tone
of its author, and to subvert what later events
imposed. When we do this, we realize that PE was a
masterpiece, not least because it tried to set a new
agenda for 20th century moral philosophy. The
historical irony of its reception consisted in
cancelling the old agenda while refusing to replace
it, as though this fulfilled all of Moore's wishes
instead of just half, indeed the wrong half, of them.
For these reasons alone, I postponed dealing with IV.
Moore's views on this topic are not made explicit
before 1912. His contributions thereafter lack
direction, and are negligible in comparison with PE
[cf. the unpublished preface to the 1922 ed.,pp.31-32
above]. Yet, we are still obliged to remove or
repair the contradiction just discovered in the 1922
paper. How best to accomplish this? Let's examine
the alternatives.

    1. We could simply throw out quote XVIII (and
its verbal follow-up) as an anomaly. Such tactics
don't merit much space.

2. We could revise our understanding of quote XVIII by invoking a technicality. No "logical law" permits us to deduce the principle of the IVI, but perhaps this is because the IVI is axiological rather than logical (Hartman redivivus). However, this is contrary to the spirit of the last three pages of the 1922 essay.

3. We could explain XVIII as a denial, not of the IVI but of some closely related yet distinguishable assertions. Let's begin by restating the several forms of the IVI given above [on p. 95], this time in our own words:

o1. An object Ø always has the same value at all times and in all places (or else it doesn't have any IV).

o2. If Ø and ØØ have different "intrinsic natures" and (therefore) different IVs, then Ø and ØØ by themselves must have the same IV, respectively.

o3. If Ø has IV, then, if ØØ = Ø, ØØ has the same IV as Ø.

o4. If Ø has IV and ØØ does not, then Ø and ØØ must be different objects.

Now let's comment on each of these. Def. o1 is a Galilean-style posit. Take it or leave it; better still, withhold judgment until it bears intangible fruit. Def. o3 is a direct consequence of o1; so is def. o4. Def. o2 is tricky, not least because Moore flounders whenever he tries to discriminate between different types of intrinsicality [CIV, 275]. But in a way it reaffirms NF versions (5) and (6): only if two objects are distinct from one another can they be self-identical. Hence, what applies to the indiscernibility of one object from itself, applies serially to each of them, in relation to one another. So o2, far from being a corollary of o1, is actually a broader application of the same underlying principle: <u>every value is what it is, anad not another value.</u> Moore's moorings are still Butlerian, after nineteen years' elapse. (That is why Moore's post-PE productions cannot be ignored or treated diffidently. Too many ideas square with one another and are sustained over long periods for us to throw out the ones which inconsiderately clash.) Hence o2, far from being a corollary of o1, is actually the most general enunciation of the IVI. Of course, o3 and o4 are far easier to grasp: o3 says that things equal in value to the same thing are equal to each other, while o4 says that things unequal to each other in value are unequal to each other. o3 and o4 are each other's contrapositive. And both are classical, so neat and so symmetrical that one is tempted to make either one of them the fundamental axiom, figuring out ways to derive all three remaining formulas from it. But I will not tamper with Moore's preferred arrangement.

Now, what is it that we are not permitted to deduce? To reword quote XVIII succinctly:

~L. if Ø has IV and ØØ is exactly like Ø, it does not follow that ØØ has (the same) IV as Ø.

Doesn't this contradict o3 (and by implication, the other three versions of the IVI)? If so, then supervenience is pitted against the overtly metaphysical strategy of finding value axioms true (or valid) in all PWs. Then the 1922 essay at first commits a subtle variant of the supernaturalistic fallacy [PE 118, 125], only to detect and root it out, a moment later. The anomaly thesis (in (2)) suddenly looks appealing, only because ~L. is so counter-intuitive. What reason does Moore have for denying the inference, anyway?

He reasons by analogy: "I do not see how it can be deduced from any logical law that, if a given patch of colour be yellow, then any patch which were exactly like the first would be yellow too" [CIV, 272]. But that can be readily deduced! (Unless 'exactly like' means 'in all other respects but this one,' in which case the non-inference is a trivial tautology, based on the (now) assumed difference between the two color patches. But see below, for a reworking of this proposal.) All this example succeeds in doing is to dispatch the fear that f/v might be resurrected: If yellow can "supervene" on lemons, roses, or sense-data, then why recoil at moral or aesthetic super-venience? Only a nominalist would still find such "non-naturalism" repugnant. It wouldn't be worth the bother to critique such an ontology or its epistemology. But there are still two drawbacks here. It makes Moore look dumb. Plus, we have done nothing to enhance the plausibility of the claim that ~L. is not directly antagonistic to any members of the set o1, o2, o3, or o4.

4. To rescue Moore from unintelligibility, let's try once more to stipulate a new reading of quote XVIII:

(M1) If two objects are identical in value, it follows that they are identical in all other respects.
(M2) If two objects are identical in all other respects, it does <u>not</u> follow that they are identical in value, nor is it always true.

(M1) is Moore's tribute to the IVI. It retracts nothing, qualifies nothing. (M2) states that the converse of the IVI (a) does not follow from the IVI, (b) does not hold in all cases. Point (a) is simply a matter of logic. Point (b) solicits a supportive counter-example. Three such instances come to mind, the first two of which are instructive yet unsuccessful. The third redeems Moore.

IX.1 The referents of 'the third prime number' and 'the integer that precedes four' are identical. Yet plainly neither of them has value. So it is misleading to refer to them as "identical in value," since wrong with grouping solecisms together?

Objection: But their value <u>is</u> identical-- namely, none. What's misleading (or rule-exceptional) about that?

Reply: Nothing. It's defeated. Try again.

IX.2 The standard meter stick in Paris and another meter stick, made of the same metal, heated to the same temperature and kept under the same conditions in Hoboken, are identical in all respects. Yet only the Parisian meter stick has value, because it has been adopted as the unit of length by which all the others are to be measured.

Objections: (a) These two meter sticks aren't really identical since they are located in different places.

Reply: Granted, but does spatio-temporal distinctness have any genuine bearing on these issues? Moore's own criteria for identity are largely semantic, as we know from PGEM (1942), exchange with Langford concerning the "paradox of analysis" [cf. O'Connor (1982), 76-77, 80-83 and Klemke (1969B), 83-87]. In the 1922 essay he is mum, so we have no idea how stringent or lax his requirements might be. If two recordings (or auditions) of Beethoven's Fifth Symphony are separated in time or by successive playings, does this really affect value-comparisons between them? What about the same recording, played twice in a row? Granted, the auditor's mood may be different on each occasion. In particular, the second hearing may be modified (or enriched) by insights gleaned from the first hearing. But nothing prevents the experiences from being "the same" in principle, as Moore even suggests at the very end of his 1932 paper (PP, 100). If IX.1 hadn't been shot down so quickly, one would be tempted to avoid the problem by dealing exclusively with abstract entities. This may still be feasible, provided one chooses one's (onto)logical weapons carefully.

(b) The decision to let the Paris meter stick be the basis for measurement is an arbitrary convention. Why couldn't it be in Hoboken, instead? The OQA pertains to this situation.

Reply: That would demonstrate the fatuity of the OQA better than anything I could bring against it. But this objection is irrelevant, since if the OQA does apply, then we are forever stuck with the negative insights of PE Chap. I, and no theory of IV, let alone an enunciation of the IVI, would stand a chance. Why bother? (And why pay attention to Moore, or to any philosopher who (incongruously) did care enough to bother? No wonder that "philosophy always buries its undertakers" [Putnam (1983), 303, quoting Gilson].

(c) Meter sticks don't have intrinsic value, but only instrumental value.

Reply: I think Moore would agree, although they are nice to gaze at sometimes. The comparison is inappropriate, hence dismissed. So much for measurement!

IX.3 What about (e.g.) a work of art in relation to a copy or expert forgery of same? Doesn't the former have intrinsic value, the latter, none? Notwithstanding objection (a) to counter-example IX 2, isn't this the sort of puzzle that vindicates Moore in blocking the (biconditional) inference from identity to identity of value?

Reply: Yes. Consider Goodman's account of "the perfect fake" [Goodman (1968), 99]. Just what makes two pictures "differ aesthetically" [Ibid., 109], although "...nobody, not even the most skilled expert, can ever tell the pictures apart by merely looking at them" [Ibid., 101]? Goodman avers that total failure to discriminate between the pictures does not preclude becoming able to distinguish between them at some future date [Ibid., 102]. True, but this is an epistemic consideration, thus irrelevant to the hypothesis as stated. Hence, Goodman reformulates the question: "...suppose it could be proved that no one ever will be able to see any difference?" [Ibid., 106; G.s italics and punctuation]. His reply is that this cannot be proved, both for "technological reasons" [Ibid., 107] and inasmuch as the varieties of (humanly) perceptible qualia are well-nigh infinite, as Hume showed for the case of the 'missed shade of blue.' This too is an evasion, unless Goodman means that no two pictures could be identical, unless they were the same picture. In that case, he has solved the problem by arguing in a circle. Goodman would have been better off had he appropriated the IVI, instead of tacitly appealing to Leibniz' law. For the "sameness" of two picture-experiences is not (merely) a physical relation between two objects, but a recurrent organic unity involving no fewer than four participants: objects A and B, which are looked at, and respective agents C and D, which look at them. Whether A = B (or C = D) is not the decisive factor; the equivalence obtains, if at all, between the respective links connecting A-C with B-D. I may look at one and the same painting, on two discrete occasions, without enjoying the same (or similar) uplift. Conversely, you and I may stare intently at two different paintings, yet undergo the same kind of transport, whether we experience it together or separately, contemporaneously or 500 years apart. Likewise, Moore refuses to license the inference from identity simpliciter to value-identity. A tempting move, but one which Moore rightly resists as fallacious. Even if two paintings (or songs) were exactly alike in every respect except spatial (temporal) location, it would not follow that they "mean as much" to two different experiences, or even to the same agent judging at a given moment. Such language isn't even appropriate in this context. Moreover, Moore's finicky logic is by no means a corollary of supervenience or an indirect justification for it, since it neither entails nor supports the claim that attributions of value are groundless, that they bear no logical relation to facts. That interpretation goes to the opposite extreme, committing an error which Moore consistently avoided, thanks precisely to his long-standing reliance on the POU, as in PE. At last we are able to see the wisdom of Moore's scruples, despite the sterility of his analogies and his lack of imagination. Even if prolonged scrutiny of IX.3 were to show no violation of (M1), (M2) would still be necessary and justified.

It is therefore possible to reconcile Moore's statements with themselves, to preserve and even add to his initial list of value-axioms, without running into insuperable contradictions. His "non-naturalism" is domesticated into a set of logical "if...then" relationships, to expand on what we barely get to glimpse in 1903. In spirit, though not in (axio)logical letter, this isn't so far from Hartman's Cantorian recommendations. Eventually, Moore concedes that if a state of affairs is good, it follows that there is some experience (of good) taking place in the world [PGEM 618]. On one hand, this belatedly admits that values logically imply facts, full recognition of which might have made Moore convert from a "reluctant" to an enthusiastic naturalist. On the other hand, what Moore concedes is a straightforward consequence of the POU and the IT. Consciousness must be merged with its (intentional) object, to derive or obtain maximum possible goodness (or beauty) from various situations, both real and hypothetical. There are two Moores: one who doesn't follow through on his own most trenchant theses, and one who prevents them from surfacing! Fortunately, Moore doesn't heed either voice all the time, or allow one to drown out the other. This makes purging Moore of misunderstandings, misstatements and self-denials both fascinating and an endless project. What will be left when this task is complete? Nothing less than a pioneer contribution to modality, as the underlying conception of value-theory. Given Moore's standing interest in (and influence on) deontology, this isn't surprising. But given his announced opposition to metaphysical ethics, it is a marvel and a wonder that he managed to overcome his own stubbornness, to experiment with new thoughts while continuing to profess all of the old ones. Moore is like an old flying ace who sends his machine straight into the storm, defying both nature and self-preservation. Sometimes he crashes. But his ideas survive, in pieces if not intact. And there will always be a few enthusiasts and collectors, to keep them on display.

We have fulfilled the promise to vindicate Moore's world-class reputation. IVI entails facts, and enables values to lie along the axiological continuum. The rift is healed. Naturalism and non-naturalism converge. At last we attain peace and unity. But not for long. Accordingly, it's time to take stock. What have we accomplished, and do we have a right to be confident of our own conclusions? If Moore's own career teaches us anything, it's the need for relentless self-scrutiny. Hence, we should do no less for ourselves than for the texts we have just investigated. The chapter next begins this process.

CHAPTER X

FACING THE VALUES

1. Preamble

Two general results emerge from this study. The first, in light of everything we have argued from Chapter I on, is that "to escape normativeness is, therefore, impossible" [Najder (1975), 122]. The second is that Moore is partially aware of this, and (perhaps unwittingly) helps to establish this proposition and refute its denial [cf. pp. 80-82]. As we follow the course of PE, we discover, too, that the official reading of Moore (p. 19) is wrong and inadequate, but understandably so. Moreover, the label "non-naturalist" does neither itself nor Moore any justice. Moore's complexity, from beginning (OQA) to end (quotes XVII and XVIII) permits no simple categorizations. He is ambiguous, difficult, obstinate, slow to see the implications of his own work, and plagued by self-doubt. Simultaneously, these are his greatest virtues! Once we grasp these points, understanding of and tolerance for Moore increase, and previous value-polemics diminish or no longer ensue. Contrary to what I used to think, progress in value-theory does not depend on finding ways to browbeat the OQA. Defeating Moore is not a prelude to abandonment. Rather, progress will come only when we appreciate PE sufficiently to extend and incorporate its best ideas, while we proceed to formulate our own.

2. Meeting the Opposition Half-Way

The reader may agree that the textbook version of Moore is unfaithful to PE, yet remain suspicious of my philosophical claims concerning the untenability of the f/v dichotomy. It would be unreasonable to deny that we need the f/v distinction for certain purposes, regardless of its defects. How else can we approve of peace and not of war, or avoid confusing the real with the idea? Why can't we grant that f/v has heuristic power or merit, even if it does engender insoluble paradoxes when pressed too far?

One way of doing this is to follow Karl Popper's lead. Popper, in a set of Addenda to the 5th edition of The Open Society and Its Enemies, differentiates between facts and standards, alleging an "asymmetry" between these concepts [Popper (1966), Vol. II, 384]. This is not the f/v dichotomy in a different verbal guise. Popper stresses that "...standards always pertain to facts," while "...facts are evaluated by standards" [Popper (1966), Vol. II, 384; P.s italics]. Both facts and standards are governed by a "regulative idea" [Ibid., 385], so that no proposal occurring in either domain is ever infallible, or beyond criticism. "Absolute truth" is a "...model for the realm of standards" [Ibidem], an ideal to be sought, but never achieved. It helps us to correct and profit from our mistakes, "...to lift ourselves by our own bootstraps" [Ibid., 386]. The only difference between facts and standards is that we "...create our standards by proposing, discussing and adopting them" [Ibid., 385; P.s italics], whereas with "...the decision to accept a proposition we do not create the corresponding fact" [Ibid., 384; P.s italics].

There is much to commend in Popper's analysis. Even his defense of a "dualism" of facts and standards [Ibid., 392] does not resurrect the f/v dichotomy, but merely calls attention to the need to "transcend" what we accept as truth at any given moment. This is in keeping with Popper's account of scientific method, which emphasizes the role of falsifiability, of disconfirmation of theories, and of "conjectures and refutations" as the source of intellectual growth and problem-solving capacity. If this is tantamount to a f/v dichotomy, then it is one that I can live with. Moreover, the claim that we do not create facts is simply Popper's expression for the independence of the real from what we hope, wish for or desperately want to believe [cf. pp. 6-7]. Popper trades on the ambiguity between "facts" and their referents. Since facts are subject to evaluation and revision, are guided by regulative ideas of truth, and are in part the product of standards which pertain to them, Popper's own words commit him to a dialectic of fact/standard--the furthest thing imaginable from a f/v disjunction. No reluctant naturalist, he.

Popper's argument in opposition to fact/standard "identity" [Ibid., 393] and in support of an uncrossable "gulf" has a familiar sound: "We can always ask whether a development as here described ...was 'good' or 'bad'" [Ibid., 392; P.s quote-marks]. Whether Popper knowingly borrowed

Moore's OQA or reinvented it to suit his own purposes, is beside the point. What makes his conception work is that we are entitled to be as critical of facts as of standards, and critical in the same way. Knowledge is advanced (only) through error elimination; verisimilitude lasts for as long as each of our hypotheses has not died in our stead. Popper claims to be defending the "autonomy" of value [Ibid., 385], but what he really means is that no proposition (whether about a fact or a standard) can claim ultimacy for itself. Popper has taken Goedel's incompleteness theorem to his bosom, but in a manner radically different from Moore's own anticipation of Goedel [cf. Rohatyn (1982B), and pp 26, 46-47, above]. The infinite regress aspect of the OQA doesn't embarrass Popper. To the contrary, he revels in it. That is why he can use it without being destroyed by it--his methodology thrives and is based on human adversity, i.e., the permanently uncertain and adventurous character of thought and experience. Like Dewey and Peirce, Popper derives support and inspiration from evolutionary no less than from democratic theory, to crystallize and establish his position. Like Mill, Popper deeply feels the need for fallibility, whereas Moore is barely able to cerebralize it once [PE 20]. The positive insights of PE Chap. VI are as final and dogmatic in tone as their negative Chapter I counterparts were. This almost nullifies the charm of Moore's self-opposition. It also undoes the stereotype of Moore as self-effacing and open-minded. Moreover, "in matters of intrinsic value, Moore is a dogmatist," whereas "in matters of duty, he is skeptic" [Levi (1974), 274]. This is odd, though not contradictory. For these reasons, Moore and Popper contrast very sharply in temperament, despite a superficial ideological compatibility between them.

In any case, the reader who is not convinced by my account, or who persists in maintaining, both that "value includes fact" and that "value is independent of fact" [Hall (1952), 249], may find Popper's analysis more satisfactory. Indeed, so do I! It gratifies our intellectual demand for an is-ought contrast without hardening it into a linguistic barrier, logical taboo or ontological divide. Its secret is simple: it treats is-ought gaps no differently from is-is, or ought-ought. There are no unconditional truths or principles, but only an unending dialogue between expectations and consequences, with the scientific community acting as self-correcting mediator. Every proposition states conditions to be fulfilled by experience. Hence, every proposition is simultaneously both normative and predictive. We revise some prescriptions in thanks to the failure of nature or society to conform to them. Just as every hypothesis is tentative, so too the dictates of the human will are always provisional. This "duality" of facts/standards is Popper's version of respect for objectivity, which has obvious repercussions for the proper conduct of politics, no less than of science. Perfection is striven for but never reached; death is the sole equilibrium available to individuals. Nor is this cause for Sisyphean despair. The mature person takes comfort and pride in measuring the cumulative distance the species has traversed, though realizing that the road not travelled remains infinite in length.

3. Whose Fallacy?

A desperate attempt to save Moore from the force of (his own) criticism might begin by re-examining the logic on which the OQA founders. In an interesting and thorough essay, Douglas Walton and Lynn Batten contend that the traditional fallacy of arguing in a circle is not clear-cut [Walton and Batten (1984), 148-152]. Their discussion is indirectly relevant to Moore, and therefore worth pursuing here.

Circular argument (petitio principii) is usually defined as assuming what should be proved, or else as smuggling one or more key premises into an argument that have not been accepted in advance by all parties. The aim of such deception is to generate a conclusion that the argument might not otherwise yield, while concealing the lack of independent verification to support the assumptions blithely made. Ever since J.S. Mill, logicians have worried that begging the question might not be a fallacy, since mathematical deductions and harmless tautologies alike appear to be guilty of committing it. But begging the question is usually classed as an informal, not a formal, fallacy. An argument may be valid, even sound, and yet fallacious if it cheats (e.g.) by introducing rules which are controversial rather than commonplace. Arguments which conclude that abortion is morally wrong (right) on the grounds that the fetus is (not) a person, or which tell us to vote for (or against) X on the grounds that the

political party to which (s)he belongs is by
definition competent (or corrupt), are cases in
point.

None of this upsets Walton and Batten, however.
Their concern is with a perceived limitation on the
right to inquire. They sense some arbitrariness
affecting the logical conditions under which debate
takes place. They therefore wonder what entitles the
disputatants even to agree to forbid (viciously)
circular arguments, or to exclude them from
ratification: "Why should the respondent be
restricted to querying propositions he does not
accept? And why should he have the right to demand
only propositions in response that he does accept?
Should not the opponent have the right to 'try
out'responses that the respondent may or may not
accept?" [Ibid., 148; authors' quote-marks]. If we
view logical argument and the give-and-take of
question and answer as a game, whose objective is to
persuade at least one of the participants to believe
a certain thesis, then "Why is that the only
legitimate sort of dialectical game?" [Ibidem]. Why
can't we opt out? The authors conclude that the
standard account of petitio principii "...does not
tell us what is wrong with arguing in a circle"
[Ibid., 149], but merely that if we want to play the
argument game with one or more partners, we must
abide by its (or their) rules. This can never
"...tell us why a game of this sort is the only one
that is permissible" [Ibidem]. In sum, the rule
against begging the question "...begs or at least
postpones the question" [Ibidem]! With this deft
self-referential critique behind them, the authors
easily draw the needlessly cautious conclusion that
"...many allegations of circularity are harder to
defend and less worrisome than the Standard Treatment
of the textbooks would have us believe" [Ibid., 163].

Several reactions to this over-ingenious line of
thought are called for:

(a) If begging the question is not a fallacy,
then the OQA is a bogeyman, suitable for scaring
small minds but not (presumably) grown philosophers.
And then there is nothing to fear from PE Chap. I. It
is only a pity that we have taken Moore to heart, or
that I have wasted my and your time by continuing to
take his jibes seriously. Indeed,if begging the question is not a fallacy, then we may rest easy about a
great many other things that used to disturb us.

(b) Communication must start somewhere, lest it become impossible or degenerate into random noise. Perhaps a given rule is willful or arbitrary, but rules in general are not, except in being products of social conventions. The OQA is a rule, too; its presence inhibits us in certain ways, even by being mentioned. Unlimited questioning is no more anarchic than other modes of game-playing. Linguistic anarchy, even if conceivable, is just another game. In any case, discourse cannot be prolonged without adhering to a framework of (tacit) rules; the sole alternative is silence.

(c) Significantly, all of the arguments quoted by Walton and Batten against the thesis that begging the question constitutes a fallacy employ the OQA in its purest form: the unlimited repetition of "why?" This shows several things:

(i) If the OQA is valid, then not just ethics but rationality in general is invalid. Even saying this is self-contradictory, since we must have some standards by which to assess invalidity--and those (perforce) constitute rationality! No wonder that the OQA isn't worth losing any sleep over; it disproves too much.

(ii) Since the alleged problem with the rule prohibiting begged questions is that it too begs the question, either the rule does not violate any logical canon (since begging the question isn't a legitimate complaint any more), or else we are tacitly appealing to the rule in objecting to it. So the rule must take on a more absolute character than before--an immutable essence misrepresented by a succession of flawed verbal appearances.

(iii) Self-reference works against Walton and Batten; despite their cleverness, they are compelled to play "the game" in the act of disassociating themselves from it. At most, they can say that the <u>formulation</u> of the law outlawing circular argument is defective; anything stronger is automatically self-defeating. If it's wrong to adopt "begging the question" because it begs the question to do so, then the law is not being challenged, merely reaffirmed at a higher level. This merely strengthens the case for the absoluteness of <u>petitio principii</u> as an inviolable law, without which discourse becomes chaotic.

fitting complement to the parallels between Moore and Goedel.

It won't do to say that the authors are in transition from one linguistic paradigm to another, or that their appeal to the opposition is only temporarily couched in the enemy's terms, to facilitate understanding. Such rules unintentionally disclose a shared set of communicative rules, which continue to operate in the very act of trying to circumvent them, and which we unavoidably appeal to, grasp, and accept in the very process of undermining them. Total incommensurability demands total silence. Anything less entails partial intertranslatability, hence, mutual respect for certain axioms undeniably held in common. The Sophists (Gorgias, Euthydemus) exploited this, whereas contemporary theorists of discourse (Grice, Habermas, Barth and Krabbe) attempt to codify it.

Walton and Batten have no stake in the OQA, yet their identically reasoned argument reproduces it on a global scale, warts and all. This actually makes it easier to follow, and we may be more receptive to a critique which is not tied to Moore's (or our) major concerns. Walton and Batten succeed in showing that the conception of logic as "value-neutral" is pure humbug. Logic belongs to a social and rhetorical domain which is saturated with values and value-commitments. The question is never whether we shall or should have values, but which ones are logically unavoidable. This transcendental point was missed by Wittgenstein, who was too preoccupied with relativism to see where "forms of life" must lead [cf. Apel (1980), 255]. By indirect proof, we arrive at binding norms which are inescapable (universal) and logically prior to the rules that they make possible [cf. the Kantian reconstruction on pp. 91-92]. This happens inadvertently in Walton and Batten's case; they push their objections against rules to a limit beyond which they themselves cannot go. Such boundaries ground or prove the primacy of certain values. Yet, life does not become noticeably easier as a result; in the presence of real-life ambiguities, we are usually confused, muddled, and pained about what to do. Good and evil, right and wrong are not easily segregated, and applying gray matter to gray areas rarely can count on apodictic proof (or disproof) to help decide the case. No wonder that Moore trembles over the opprobrious task of assigning duties in PE Chap. V. No one is

(iv) What about the OQA? It too state[s (what it] depends on) a rule--and why adopt that? Any [rule] limits us, i.e., conditions or compels one or [more] subsequent choices. The logic of selection [thus] constrains God, let alone mortals (p. 65). [The] alternative is to have no rules--which correspo[nds] either to the imagined state of the universe "bef[ore]" the Big Bang or else to an anti-game in which [the] sole rule is to have none. This paradox qui[etly] determines the limits of possible discourse [cf. [i] above].

Here we find the similarity between Walton, Batten, and G.E. Moore. Indefinite repetition [of] "why?" is itself an ultimate rule of procedure, to [be] followed religiously, even while (or precise[ly] because) we terrorize all of its ethical victims wi[th] the threat of incompleteness. Now apply the OQA [to] itself, and it degenerates into an arbitrary posi[tion] no better, no worse (on its own terms) than a[ny] others that we might try. Fail or refuse to app[ly] it, and it becomes guilty of hypocrisy, or simpl[e] inconsistency. Since no other possibilities ar[e] available, the OQA necessarily collapses, or i[s] liable to the charge that it conceals a double standard--one for itself, one for its rivals. This may be what Walton and Batten intend to convey. If so, their article performs a service, by vindicating the self-referential destruction of the OQA, as we have alleged. If the OQA is not turned against itself, then its scope is restricted, it is shamefully exempt from its own demands, and subject to counter-example. It is harmless unless it is all-inclusive; but as soon as it becomes the latter, it bars itself. Weakened, it becomes another heuristic device, something applicable, sometimes not. Strengthened, it acquires tremendous power, but is ultimately self-defeating.

(v) The anti-fallacy debunking practiced by Walton and Batten exhibits the same oddity. (The following dilemma assumes that fallacies trespass upon inviolable rules of reasoning. If fallacies are context dependent, my initial premise poses a false dichotomy. But this subtlety does not affect my main point.) If begging the question isn't always a fallacy, it is never a fallacy; there is no middle ground. If it's always a fallacy, then to beg the question is to commit a mistake. If it's never a fallacy, then how can begging the question be held against itself? This self-referential paradox is a righteous, least of all those who count themselves righteous.

That may account for the widespread use of the misnomer 'value-neutral.' This expression concerns actions, situations and propositions about which we are, for better or worse, relatively confident, such that problems appear settled, ends agreed-upon, norms are taken for granted, life is made manageable. There is something to be gained by studying the OQA in an area which is fresh, unexplored, emotionally less charged, and freer of rigid habits of thought and association than where it resides. The final irony of Walton and Batten's critique is that it aimed to reduce the inventory of fallacies, rather than increase their number. Are we likewise potential victims of our own heavy-handed treatment of f/v? Let's find out.

4. **Is Denial of the Fact/Value Dichotomy Self-Refuting?**

If norms (values) are logically prior to logic, then it may not be too hard to endorse the independently supported claim that values are logically prior to facts [pp. 1-10]. One question inevitably intrudes: then mustn't logic be logically prior to itself? Isn't that absurd, too? At the very least, doesn't it create an endless hierarchy of meta-rules, constantly leapfrogging each other while alternately occupying positions of rational supremacy and subservience? Hence, doesn't my critique of the OQA entail losing oneself in the same regressive vortex as Moore, or his many imitators? That would rudely upset all of our pretensions to definitive criticism, even if we cannot resurrect Moore's original position to its former pre-eminence. It would also mean that the denial of the f/v dichotomy was in as much logical trouble as the dichotomy itself--rather like the eight hypotheses Plato entertains in the *Parmenides*, which mutually deny and cancel each other out. Our triumph over Moore's OQA would then be both hollow and purchased at the most extreme expense. A fitting poetic climax for one who lives by the self-referential sword!

We could have posed this dilemma at the very beginning; but we were not ready for it then. Fortunately, the intervening discussion may guide us in seeking worthwhile, non-glib answers. The easiest reply strategy is to embrace infinity as a joyous task, as Popper does. The unstoppable (Goedelian) character of thought is then a welcome challenge, not an embarrassment. It explains why science does not stagnate, why democracy is preferable to other options, and why the riddle of life is a perpetual riddle. This is not enough, however. For we can always ask, "Why have science? Why live in an open society? Why bother to live at all?" Indeed, we would be unfaithful to Popper's (or Moore's) Socratic mandate if we did not raise these objections. Of course, a purely verbal solution is always possible, and it sounds like this: You couldn't even ask this question unless you were committed to dialogue with your fellow humans; hence, the norm of finding ways to live together with others and to promote peace and harmony is logically inescapable, no matter how (often) we choose to ignore it. Language itself entails commitment to certain values, and the wars, murders and cruelty practiced throughout history are merely signs of our weakness, cowardice and irrationality, executed in perverse defiance of what is self-evident upon inspection. Psychologically, we remain a mystery to ourselves, but logically, transcendentally, we have all the correct answers. Our failure to be virtuous does not indict our theories, but only ourselves.

This tactic provides a nice way of handling a heckler in the audience, or an annoying undergraduate whose impertinence is all too pertinent. But does this response work? Or does it contain a subtle flaw? Clearly it has an impressive group of backers, who trot out this thesis whenever convenient. Socrates shows Thrasymachus that on the latter's own terms, justice is more profitable than power and self-aggrandizement, and that the unjust person is both unhappy and at odds with himself [Republic Bk. I, 352A-354A]. Kant's famous test-cases of the categorical imperative (suicide, lies, broken promises) establish the moral law as exceptionless and self-validating [Foundations of the Metaphysics of Morals, Chapter II]. Josiah Royce argues that fragmentary forms of human fidelity to a given cause which do not serve the most inclusive ends of universal loyalty are inherently contradictory [The Philosophy of Loyalty, Chapter VIII, section iv]. And C.I. Lewis' arguments against f/v separation [see pp. 14-16], likewise ground a set of similar conclusions, in morals and politics. These doctrines are wonderful, yet they fail to stir or rouse most people to take appropriate action. Is that merely because we are morally blind, weak or sinful? Not necessarily. Consider Spinoza's conception of a free man, one who meditates on life, not on death [Ethics IV, prop. 67]. In what does such freedom consist? Simply in knowing that (s)he is not free, so that (s)he may accept the inevitable with grace. A paradox, but only because 'freedom' involves a thought-experiment, not an actual or possible condition. Hence, the disparity between our reach and our grasp. Here lies the clue to our sense of emptiness when confronting high-toned philosophical themes. What we say may be true in every case, yet we either preclude hope or else make rendering effort to achieve self-realization unnecessary. The choice is between importance or superfluity, with nothing in between, inducing Hamlet-like paralysis. Perhaps a leap of faith can break out of this verbal circle, but then where shall we jump? The existentialist view of the human predicament is that choice is groundless; hence, we can never give ourselves advice, or have any advance assurances about life. This is no better, certainly no different, than calling logic "arbitrary," as though it were capricious.

Pragmatism offers an alternative, both to tranquility and resignation. For life is nothing but a series of risks, and one's sense of adventure (if not our immediate needs) induces us to keep on placing the bets. No particular faith is reliable, except for the abstraction of having faith. This coincides with William James' conception of faith as willingness to act on behalf of an uncertain outcome, knowing that one may perish. The need to remake experience "congruously with our spontaneous powers" also enables us to go on "moral holiday" rather than suffer exhaustion, without leaving the future entirely up to Providence. Like Emerson, James tried to shake Americans out of our lethargy. Hence, he appealed to our dormant or muted impulses. Taken out of its rhetorical context, James' celebration of the life process renders a theory of organismic imperatives superfluous. Let's pursue this momentarily, paying due regard neither to history nor to James' admirable motives. Then the conundrum is as follows: If I must believe in something, then there's no point in urging me to believe it. Just as James chided hard determinists for seeking to persuade auditors that nothing can be helped, so we might tease James for making a virtue of instinctual necessity. Ought implies can—which entails that value implies fact, in this case a modal fact. Unfortunately, turning traditions, doctrines and shibboleths against themselves offers Moore's constructive program little help or consolation. For if we cannot determine what our duties are, then it makes no sense to espouse or frame any ideals, especially if they are meant to be means to further ends [PE 189]. Hence, the negative counsel of PE Chap. V precludes drawing the positive morals which Chapter VI enunciates.

To OQA or not to OQA, it makes no difference. If you OQA others, then (to be internally consistent) you must allow the OQA to be applied to you. If you don't OQA, then Moore will do it for (and to) you. And if you reject consistency as a standard, then you will either have nothing further to say or else (like Walton and Batten) become entangled in your own self-denials. This is how Aristotle rebuts critics of the law of non-contradiction in Metaphysics, Gamma. Yet, even Aristotle was unable to reduce his sophistical opponents to spluttering absurdity. He accused them of being insincere, i.e., unwilling and unable to live by their beliefs. He argued that they relied on the law of non-contradiction, especially in renouncing it, that is, in disagreeing with their adversaries. As Jonathan Lear observes, "Aristotle's strategy is to show that the possibility of signifying something depends upon adherence to the law of non-contradiction....A true opponent of the law of non-contradiction is robbed of the possibility of saying anything" [Lear (1980), 104, 110]. This is a transcendental argument with pragmatic ramifications: "...when a man is sufficiently confused to assert that he does not believe in the law of non-contradiction, his general behavior is a far better guide to his beliefs than his assertions" [Ibid., 113-114]. But this subtly begs the question, since actions which "contradict" utterances do not offend someone who explicitly rejects conventional logic [cf. Rohatyn (1982A), 80, 84].

Yet, these arguments fail, not because they are unfair to the enemy, but because in any contest between rationality and irrationality, the former's agonized conscience eventually indicts itself. Since the law of non-contradiction is an axiom, we realize that we are cheating (ourselves) if we so much as try to prove it. Likewise, in principle, inability to function without this law is merely an elevated ad hominem circumstantial, not an argument ad rem.

Hence, we endure defeat at the hands of our own rectitude, whereas an (imaginary) opponent suffers from no such restrictions. Just as civil disobedience takes advantage of the existence of democratic institutions to plead its (rightful) case against state encroachment and tyranny, so too the would-be deniers of the laws of logic are entitled to defense counsel--and we provide it for them! We could claim to be more virtuous than they, in light of our own greater self-awareness [cf. Bradley (1876/1927), 79], but this merely begs the question in another direction. Crazy or lazy, we cannot rid ourselves of such pests without violating our own standards of propriety, or stooping to the level of would-be adversaries.

The upshot of this is that in philosophy, every thesis is self-invalidating, true if and only if false. Its antitheses suffer the same aporia, as we dance in an endless circle of questions, a mounting spiral of non-definitive answers. [For a contemporary analysis of perennial dialectical conflict, see Rescher (1985).] Hegel's drunken spirit grins down lasciviously at us, and his lewd laughter resounds through time and in the corridors of the brain.

Is there no way out of this morass? Are we forced to side both with and against ourselves, simultaneously? Is the denial of the f/v dichotomy as vulnerable to criticism as its opposite number? Are we bound to acknowledge an infinite regress of opinions, without the consolation available to mathematics, where undecidability does not impair the genuineness of its theorems? Does the repudiation of f/v end up by reinstalling a distinction between philosophically provable and unprovable propositions nothing belonging in the former category, thanks to the OQA? Does the demise of the OQA (also courtesy of the OQA) forbid us to use the expression 'provably unprovable'? Is it intellectually dishonest (not just mistaken) to pretend that honesty is not just a value, but an inescapable logical "fact" (principle)? So, is writing this (or any) philosophical work an unwitting exercise in the construction of self-defeating antinomies? Is philosophy dead? Or am I merely suffering from a severe case of the Rorty blues, sometimes diagnosed as Derrida's doldrums, accompanied by MacIntyre fever?

5. The Frankfurt Connection

The dour sentiments just expressed are not the last word, for many reasons. First, we can't go back to the way things were before. The development of self-consciousness is irreversible; hiding from oneself proves futile. Second, the f/v dichotomy is defunct, regardless of the fate of its dialectically paired successors. Third, in philosophy, words are (a substitute for) actions. The OQA asks (in effect), "Why should I be moral?" to which the OQA furnishes a ready reply: "Why not?" Clever self-referential ripostes are tedious even when they are seriously meant. We may agree with Hume that pleasure is a bona-fide source of renewed philosophizing [A Treatise of Human Nature, Bk. I, Part iv, section 7; Hume (1739-40/1888), 271], yet it is difficult to believe the meaning of life consists in the treadmill-like pursuit of meaning. If that meaning cannot be grounded, then the search for it is by definition futile. (Besides, the mental pleasures afforded by philosophy cannot be identified with 'good,' to revert to the NF.)

Like Lewis, Nozick and Putnam, K.-O. Apel observes that the main doctrines of "analytical meta-ethics" form a mutually inconsistent set [Apel (1980), 241, 245, quoting Lenk]. But this is only a first step. The second concretizes speech by locating "...human utterances in the pragmatic context" [Apel (1980), 246] of deliberation, decision-making and conduct. The third is to "emancipate" ourselves by setting up "reflexive self-understanding" as an "ethical regulative" [Apel (1980), 285].

Restated in plain English: The Founding Fathers said that all men were created equal. They closed one or both eyes to slavery and the condition of women. Yet, their words are significant, since without them neither they nor we could ever be accountable for subsequent failure to live up to them. The "principle of potential moral self-transcendence" [Apel (1980), 285] means seeing through our own lies, illusions and rationalizations which alike protect the status quo; thereby ending (or fighting against) policies which perpetuate false consciousness. A phony universal is better than none at all--but it is still phony. To become genuine, we must transform it from being a document to being real, from paper guarantee to global institution and way of life. This requires a new mind-set, i.e., a commitment to revolutionary practices. It also requires technical expertise, to avoid the pitfalls of bureaucracy and other objective dangers (such as greed, power-lust, the inertia of tradition and fear) that block its realization.

The f/v dichotomy is not only of no help in performing this task, it is an obstacle which we must remove, before we can fulfill Marx's injunction to change the world, to create a more humane political and social order. To justify dismantling the f/v barrier, consider these points:

i. Science claims to be value-neutral. That is a joke. Science is shot through with values, both as a method of inquiry and as an organ of social control. It couldn't exist for one moment unless scientists and non-scientists alike continued to support, respect and utilize its goals. The responsibility of scientists is not just an "external" matter, related to science's role in human culture, but an "internal" affair, part of the activity of doing science and the standards by which scientific work is (to be) carried out [cf. Mitroff (1974), and Chapter III above]. Science is purposive: predictably so, for when it banishes final causality from its purview, it cannot witness its own teleology.

ii. Philosophy, particulary meta-ethics, claims the privilege of value-neutrality, as well. That is a joke, too, and a poor imitation of science's misplaced prerogatives. Take the study of ordinary discourse as just one example. Is it really possible to investigate (e.g.) the use of the word 'suck' in such a way that there is no overlap between its prescriptive and descriptive functions? Assuming that an "unambiguous identification of the normative" [Apel (1980), 245] were possible in each and every case, wouldn't we still have to explain why the philosopher focuses attention on certain words, indeed, why the "linguistic turn" is the major obsession of the late 20th century? The philosopher is never above the battle, least of all when (s)he employs the rhetoric of neutrality to gain converts, adherents, or some argumentative advantage over rivals within the discipline.

iii. It won't do to say that the philosopher's activity is as permeated with value-directives as that of the scientist, artist or historian. For that leaves everything exactly as before: Values are still conceived as private and "soft," facts as public and "hard". That is why the f/v dichotomy must be challenged in such a way as to restore the reputability of value-theory as a cognitive enterprise. Moreover, to exempt science from responsibility for the novel value-situations that it creates, whether through atomic weaponry, recombinant DNA, or space exploration, is (at best) to license amorality. Philosophy has no technological innovations to its credit, yet it is equally culpable for refusing or not wanting to make up for science's deficiencies. Scientists have one excuse: their training only prepares them to specialize. Philosophers, part of whose mission is to examine the human condition, have no such apologies on which to fall back. Hence, the eschewal of synoptic vision is not merely a personal failure or a symptom of individual malaise. It is a professional disgrace.

Why does it happen? Simply because philosophy is a victim of the Weberian patterns of social organization which dominate every aspect of Western life, thereby producing "reverse adaptation" [Winner (1977), 229] "or mismatch between ends and their insubordinate means." As Winner has shown, goals and norms of efficiency, productivity, hierarchical command, and (above all) fragmentation of labor create havoc, reinforce invidious distinctions between mental and manual labor, while fostering dualities of thought and emotion, separation between public and private spheres, and assorted polarities among groups and between genders [Jaggar (1983), 267, 367, 380]. We are slaves, both to our machines and to the frenetic mentality of "more, farther, faster" [Winner (1977), 315] which they project.

iv. At present, calling someone "responsible" either for causing or for being in a position to remedy the current state of things is senseless. How can we assign such responsibility when systems are so complex and interlocking, when individuals trapped inside the "iron cage" are largely powerless and unaware of the big picture, which constrains their respective roles as workers, managers, housewives, politicians--even owners of means of production? To cure all this takes nothing less than complete restructuring--which intellectuals alone cannot and should not undertake. However, we can blame

philosophers (in light of (iii) above) for being
half-witting participants in a superstructure which
covertly sanctions the lines of actual or possible
research that are approved of and kept open, the
designation of certain texts as classical or canonic
for every scholar, and the sense of legitimacy or
spuriousness surrounding 'the problems of philosophy.' The paradigm of quantitative problem-solving,
derived from science itself, is part of the
officially mandated approach to the field. Moreover,
dismissal of the foregoing critique as mere
sociology, therefore as irrelevant or genetically
fallacious, is likewise part of the apparatus by
which philosophy perpetrates self-ignorance, by
acquiescing in the larger myths which society
constructs and reproduces [cf. Willis (1981)].

Conversely, point (iv) shows us why it won't
suffice to dismiss the f/v dichotomy as a tool of
oppression, even though that is true. Nobody,
including the oppressors, feels compelled to listen.
That type of objection can be easily ridiculed as,
(a) ideologically biased, (b) special pleading, and
(c) professionally incompetent. And rightly so. Do
you simply accept an atheist's denunciation of
traditional or contemporary arguments for the
existence of God, when (s)he does not examine the
arguments dispassionately but merely fulminates about
the evils of Papal infallibility, the Inquisition and
the Crusades? Do you encourage students to substitute ad hominem arguments for calm and thorough
analysis? Would you heed what I am saying in this
section, or trouble to read further, had the diatribe
above occurred in Chapters I-III? Yes, bourgeois
conscience does make cowards of us all--but I prefer
meticulous cowardice to slovenly bravery.

Fortunately, so does Apel, who undergirds his
sociological critique by confronting f/v on its home
turf--much as Walton and Batten appeal to shared
convictions about begged questions, in order to
demonstrate to their audience that there is something
slipshod about the universal rule which forbids them.
This is excellent strategy, even if it does not
succeed. And it is refreshing, in the era of
rapprochement between European and Anglo-American
thought, to find that Dewey, Searle, Hampshire, Lewis
and Nozick have additional company. But Apel's
approach has a few flaws which he cannot hide.

(a) How can we justify the unstated but implicit presumption that all men and women <u>are</u> created equal? Is this self-evident? Does it extend to children? Or animals? Is the thesis only as broad (at any given time) as our surplus wealth, our geo-political resources and our sensitivity or sense of fair play? Must we fall back on Intuition, to defend this thesis at any level of generality? Is it susceptible to the OQA? Jurgen Habermas, who runs some nice interference on Apel's behalf, holds that "...in the power of self-reflection, knowledge and interest are one" [Habermas (1971), 314; orig. in ital.]. This is either an updated version of the arguments catalogued on (pp. 116-117,above)or else an eschatological (or utopian) prediction. If we regard it as the latter, then it is unverifiable--we will have to wait for the end of history to determine whether the conditions of "work and interaction" [Habermas (1971), 196, 288] are so adjusted that we can always act selflessly (for the best interests of humanity as a whole) without sacrificing ourselves. But there are grounds for viewing it as akin to the arguments advanced by Plato, Kant, and Royce mentioned earlier. For Habermas contends that the "reciprocal recognition of subjects" [<u>Ibid</u>., 138] is a sign of their mutual parity. This argument is tantamount to an <u>a priori</u> reconstruction of language. If the very act of communicating my intention, even an evil one, to another agent presupposes acknowledgement of the recipient as one capable of understanding and internalizing my words, then (in a twisted way) rapists, murderers and tyrants necessarily do this too. This is best evidenced by witnessing its psychological breakdown, as in Sartre's arresting depiction of a victim who implores his torturer for mercy: "...this explosion of the Other's look in the world of the sadist causes the meaning and goal of sadism to collapse. The sadist discovers that it was <u>that freedom</u> which he wished to enslave" [Sartre (1943/1964), 382; S.'s italics]. Correspondingly, we are entitled to call sadism and other such phenomena "perverse," because their continuation contradicts, mocks, and spoils the lies that their perpetrators must conceal from (and secretly admit to) themselves. Hence, the infliction of needless suffering on others is not merely wrong but stupid and irrational, exactly as Plato sometimes supposes in equating knowledge with virtue, or Kant in identifying moral law with logical consistency.

What do we say, then, when crimes against humanity go on unabated, or when Alcibiades pleads for the right to be himself [Symposium 216A] through doing so entails irreversible (self-)destruction, hence loss of the very autonomy that we cherish? We can hardly blame Habermas for human depravity. But Apel's slogan "moral self-transcendence" is problematic, since an elite class enjoys privileged educational access, i.e., to the understanding of what makes a corrupt society tick. That is why he allows no one to be a self-appointed "therapist" [Apel (1980), 285]. If revolution cannot (for the time being) be a spontaneous occurrence, while forming vanguards is barred on the grounds that they reinstitute the very class structures which obstruct or cancel human fellowship, then we have neither a necessary, nor a sufficient condition for achieving praxis. No leaders, no followers and no movement. This describes the ambivalent position of intellectuals, who know too much to stay quiet (or be bought off) yet cannot speak "for" others without objectifying them or else engaging in class-condescension. This predicament is insoluble; evading or denying it merely aggravates the problem. The intellectual's enforced paralysis indicts, not Apel, but anyone who "chooses" to revolt, but whose choice unavoidably impinges (even if it somehow avoids imposing) on others. Hence, all talk of revolt is either just talk, or else more irresponsible than the bourgeois morality it condemns.

(b) Likewise, if we appeal to the enemy on the enemy's own grounds, then, like Walton and Batten, we risk contradicting ourselves, i.e., unavoidably accepting the same norms we feign to critique and revise. If false universalizations are to be replaced by true ones, then we cannot object to universality, but only to the "gap" between what we preach and what we (or others) practice. This is the whole point of making practice align or coincide with theory. Hence, we share the same values as our opponents. This can't be shrugged off as a temporary expedient, an attention-getting device, or an attempt to cross an incommensurability divide, for reasons discussed on pp. 113-114. All such pleas fail, so that our own principles convict us of fraud or perjury (pp.118-119), without reference to any specific ideological foe. The alternatives are to capitulate or shut up.

(c) Let's grant Apel the insight that norms are irreducibly moral in content and implications, even if they purport to be purely methodological [Apel (1980), 246]. This certainly applies to the OQA, as we said in this chapter. But then there is no reason to object to norms on that score, unless they seek to escape the consequences. The OQA fails, precisely because it creates an infinite regress, a series of doubts to which it itself is liable. We can't live with it, and we can't get along or live without it, either. Commitment to a norm isn't annoying; perpetual self-erasure is. Only Popper, for whom regresses betoken health, would presume to enjoy this existence and even defend it on principle. But even that shows that the logical conundrums posed by and for the OQA establish the limits of pure reasoning and of intelligible discourse. It is unenlightening to conclude that these issues involve value commitments. They do, but so what? All this does is throw us back upon the chicken-egg question unveiled on p. 115; which comes first, logic or the "logically prior" commitment to logic? To avoid falling into a trap, the wise answer is: neither. Both logic and its tacit rules are ultimate, fundamental, inseparable constituents of meaning, of the several factors that make linguistic coherence and communicative order possible.

If value and fact are so intertwined that they cannot be pulled or split apart, then why did people (not just philosophers) ever (decide to) distinguish them? Were they simply ignorant, or part of a conspiracy? Did they wear ideological blinders, or were they company (wo)men? And if so, what are we? Do fashions which once dictated that "no one in his right mind could deny" a f/v gulf now trumpet that "no one in his right mind could affirm it" [Holmes (1981), 394]? Though the pendulum has not swung back that far, we must be leery of reductive, let alone motive-hunting, explanations. Sociology of philosophy is a worthy but as yet undeveloped project [Miller (1984), 313], one barely outlined in proposed studies of the "comparative morphology of philosophical knowledge" [Levi (1974), 309]. It must secure its ecological niche before we can trust its methodology.

In the meantime, possibly for all time, I prefer to regard the f/v dichotomy as a powerful and disturbing metaphor for the "chiasm" that separates and unites human flesh sexually, politically and (as

Merleau-Ponty (1968) explains) conceptually. We are
both one and many, same and different, angels and
animals, minds and bodies, subjects and objects.
This always ambivalent status makes us justifiably
uneasy, like the onlookers in Rembrandt's Anatomy
Lesson. To account for half-truths requires a
perspective on experience which encompasses yet
transcends them. Let us call this a metaphysics. No
metaphysics is ever adequate, for the reason just
given: humans are not gods. Yet (as Hegel saw), the
very awareness of our own mortality makes us
transfinite. Hence, every metaphysics is maddeningly
true as well as disappointingly false. Perfection
escapes us, yet imperfection is what's perfect about
us. Poetically as well as prosaically, philosophy
renews and reflects our precarious condition. Hence,
the f/v dichotomy powerfully conveys the truth about
our divided nature; whereas denying that dichotomy
seeks to make us whole. Since we are both whole and
divided, we should not deny or abolish such posits,
but rather strive to incorporate them in a larger
synthesis. Since incompleteness is our birthright,
we cannot transcend the f/v dichotomy, nor can we
overcome it by overcoming both it and its negation.
No matter how thoroughly we grasp the structure of
paradox, its essence (by definition) eludes us. Even
Goedel's famous theorem is not provably unprovable,
but depends on an indemonstrable assumption (that
arithmetic is consistent). Hence, it too is an
elegant cipher of our permanent suspension in
cognitive limbo. Yet, we need not be frustrated, for
as Tillich remarked, "that symbol is most adequate
which expresses not only the ultimate but also its
own lack of ultimacy" [quoted in Pielke (1986), 137].
Isn't this the profound depth that "fallibility" was
meant to sound? If this was what logical positivists
were really after, then it's a terrible shame that
the rhetorical excesses of the Weimar era prevented
liberal and tolerant people from opposing fascism and
objecting to Spengler's influence without undermining
all the very commitments that made it logical for
them to do so. To aspire to be value-free, one must
value freedom. How aptly the Vienna Circle named
itself.

Knowing all this transports us beyond anger.
But it does not bring instant peace or tell us how to
live. Can we find ourselves before it's too late?

6.   Life-Boat Axiology

We want so much to make a "personal contribution x" to the universe [James (1881/1977), 340], to feel that what we do matters, and that the universe is waiting for us to help perfect it. Like James, we want the world to be flexible and open, to eschew the equally predestined extremes of providence and doom, between which poles the OQA relentlessly oscillates. Is this possible, or is ours not one of those possible worlds in which our thoughts and acts can make a difference? Is Moorean contemplation of 'good' and of the good justifiable only as a refined form of hedonism? If so, then it might pattern itself after Einstein, who when asked why he continued searching for the equations describing the unified field despite a quarter century of fruitlessness, calmly replied, "Weil es mir Spass macht." Or, consider the plight of Dorothy Hare, heroine of one of George Orwell's early novels. Enmeshed in a loss of faith crisis, she ponders her fate in prolonged Dostoievskian reverie. Dorothy worries that without God:

> XIX....no possible substitute for faith; no pagan acceptance of life as sufficient unto itself; no pantheistic cheer-up stuff, no pseudo-religion of 'progress' with visions of glittering Utopias and ant-heaps of steel and concrete. Either life on earth is a preparation for something greater and more lasting, or it is meaningless, dark and dreadful...if death ends all, then there is no hope and no meaning in anything...[Orwell (1935), 316-317].

A moment later, she suddenly snaps herself out of her blue funk:

> XX. Dorothy started. She realised that she had wasted twenty minutes, and her conscience stabbed her so hard that all the questions that had been worrying her fled out of her mind. What on earth have I been doing all this time? ...come on, Dorothy! No slacking, please. You've got to get that breastplate done before supper [Orwell (1935), 318].

Note how Dorothy surmounts her crisis. The dichotomy between life and one's hopes for the after-life is surely a false one, but Dorothy does not attack her own logic directly. She believes, neither in heaven nor in bringing heaven down to earth. Her own career and social status are negligible. She chooses not to dwell on her mortality. Don't these non-intellectual performances betray her inauthenticity? Isn't she in flight from self-awareness, or being towards death? Isn't her behavior shallow, if not self-deceptive? Isn't she further proof that Orwell's female protagonists are (at best) wimps and hopeless victims of their (male-dominated) environment? Not in my eyes. On the contrary, her resolve demonstrates a renewed commitment to other people--to those in the same predicament as herself, which means, everyone. Here is the only universal which we cannot fail to exemplify. Hence, the only question is how we bear up under an affliction which is mutual, though it strikes us separately. "The solid meaning of life is always the same eternal thing--the marriage, namely, of some unhabitual ideal, however special, with some fidelity, courage, and endurance; with some man's or woman's pains" [James (1899/1977), 659]. We are all in the same boat, though we go overboard on different nights, some quietly, some shrieking. This does not deny that there are vast differences in people's lives. It merely confirms a common denominator, obvious yet excruciating to admit.

7. Coda

So it isn't necessary for us to prove that we are equal. A verse from Ecclesiastes or a jar of ashes will do. (Compare the ending of Stanley Kubrick's screen adaptation of William Thackeray's Barry Lyndon.) A great deal of thought could be saved by looking at life in the way that Dorothy does: as something that neither can nor needs to be justified. Whether we cherish or despise it, cultivate or squander it, the gift must eventually return to its source. In some cases, sooner. Whether we want life or not, at some point life doesn't want us anymore. Seeing that gets Dorothy over the hurdle.

Did Moore fathom this? Partially. With his help, we can appreciate why the OQA reflects this paradox, in poising us between value-alternatives all of which it equips us to reject, not sparing itself in the process. We can appreciate why he resorts to Intuition, as a cipher for what we do when the OQA takes root, when we neither have, need nor want reasons for willing to live, to think, to reason, to be philosophers. And so, at last we may vindicate his pronouncements about friendship and beauty, as we were unable to accomplish before. For what else is there to life, except you and me and the things we can create to touch each other inside? By freezing time and space in art and sculpture, playing with its flow and contour in music and poetry, and preserving its passage in literature and history, we immortalize our experiences, memories and feelings as though flesh were an illusion. By comparison, miracles are commonplace, and technological control, cheap.

Someday you must die your death, and I mine. Even the conjuring power of art cannot prevent this from happening. At most, it makes the throes bearable. The articulation and yes, even the suppression of individual despairs already transmogrifies them, and makes us beings toward beings. In the possible worlds in which we intervene, in the lived space which we occupy, fact and value join and meld, and cannot be rent or put asunder.

REFERENCES AND WORKS CONSULTED

Achtenberg, Deborah. "What is Goodness? An Introduction." Ph.D. dissertation, New School for Social Research, 1982.

Apel, Karl-Otto. "The A Priori of the Communication Community and the Foundations of Ethics: The Problem of a Rational Foundation of Ethics in the Scientific Age." In Towards a Transformation of Philosophy. Trans. Glyn Adey and David Frisby. London: Routledge and Kegan Paul, 1980, 225-300.

Baier, Kurt. "What Is Value? An Analysis of the Concept." In Kurt Baier and Nicholas Rescher (eds.), Values and the Future; the Impact of Technological Change on American Values. New York: Free Press, 1969, 33-67.

Bartley, William Warren, III. The Retreat to Commitment (2nd ed.). La Salle, IL: Open Court Publishing Company, 1984.

Beardsley, Monroe C. "Intrinsic Value." Philosophy and Phenomenological Research, Vol. 26 (1965); repr. in The Aesthetic Point of View. Michael J. Wreen and Donald M. Callen (eds.). Ithaca, NY: Cornell University Press, 1982, 46-64.

Bradley, Francis Herbert. Ethical Studies (1876) (2nd ed). Intro. Richard Wollheim. London: Oxford University Press, 1927.

Broad, Charles Dunbar. "G.E. Moore's Latest Published Views in Ethics." Mind, Vol. 70 (1961); repr. in Alice Ambrose and Morris Lazerowitz (eds.), G.E. Moore: Essays in Retrospect. London: Routledge and Kegan Paul, 1970, 350-373.

Butcharov, Panayot. "That Simple, Indefinable, Nonnatural Property Good." Review of Metaphysics, Vol. 36 (1982), 51-75.

Dewey, John. Theory of Valuation (International Encyclopedia of Unified Science, Vol. II, No. 4). Chicago: University of Chicago Press, 1939.

Donagan, Alan. "W.K. Frankena and G.E. Moore's Metaethics." *The Monist*, Vol. 64 (1981), 293-304.

Duncan-Jones, Austin. "Intrinsic Value: Some Comments on the Work of G.E. Moore." *Philosophy*, Vol. 33 (1958); repr. in Ambrose and Lazerowitz (eds.), *G.E. Moore: Essays in Retrospect* (q.v. under Broad, above), 304-342.

Elster, Jon. *Logic and Society. Contradictions and Possible Worlds*. Chichester and New York: John Wiley and Sons, 1978.

———. *Sour Grapes. Studies in the Subveresion of Rationality*. Cambridge: Cambridge University Press, 1983.

Feldman, Fred. *Introductory Ethics*. Englewood Cliffs, NJ: Prentice-Hall, 1978 (see esp. Chapter 13, "Moore and Non-Naturalism,"193-211).

Findlay, John Niemeyer. *Axiological Ethics*. New York: St. Martin's Press, 1970 (see esp. Chapter III, "Moore Rashdall and Ross," 37-44).

Fogelin, Robert J. *Evidence and Meaning*. New York: Humanities Press, 1967.

Frankena, William K. "The Naturalistic Fallacy." *Mind*, Vol. 48 (1939). Repr. in E.D. Klemke (ed.), *Studies in the Philosophy of G.E. Moore*. Chicago: Quadrangle Books, 1969, 30-43.

French, Peter. *The Scope of Morality*. Minneapolis: University of Minnesota Press, 1979.

Gewirth, Alan. *Reason and Morality*. Chicago: University of Chicago Press, 1978.

Goodman, Nelson. *Languages of Art; An Approach to a Theory of Symbols*. Indianapolis and New York: Bobbs-Merrill, 1968.

Habermas, Juergen. *Knowledge and Human Interests* (trans. Jeremy J. Shapiro). Boston: Beacon Press, 1971.

Hall, Everett W. *What is Value? An Essay in Philosophical Analysis*. New York: Humanities Press, 1952.

Hamblin, Charles L. Fallacies. London: Methuen, 1970.

Hampshire, Stuart. "Fallacies in Moral Philosophy." Mind, Vol. 58 (1949). Repr. in Freedom of Mind and Other Essays. Princeton, NJ: Princeton University Press, 1971, 42-63.

Hartman, Robert S. "The Definition of Good: Moore's Axiomatic of the Science of Ethics." Proceedings of the Aristotelian Society, Vol. 65 (1964-65), 237-256.

_____. The Structure of Value. Carbondale, IL: Southern Illinois University Press, 1967.

_____. "The Structure of Tertiary Qualities." In Eugene F. Kaelin (ed.), Man and Value: Essays in Honor of William H. Werkmeister. Tallahassee, FL: University Presses of Florida, 1981, 126-153.

Hartogh, Govert Den. "Practical Inference and the Is/Out Question." Journal of Value Inquiry, Vol. 14 (1980), 129-147.

Hill, John. The Ethics of G.E. Moore: A New Interpretation. Assen, Netherlands: Van Gorcum, Ltd., 1976.

Hochberg, Herbert. "Moore's Ontology and Non-natural Properties." Review of Metaphysics, Vol. 15 (1962). Repr. in Klemke (ed.), Studies in the Philosophy of G.E. Moore (1969) (q.v. above, under Frankena), 95-127.

Hollinger, Robert. "Can a Scientific Theory Be Legitimately Criticized, Rejected, Condemned or Suppressed on Ethical or Political Grounds?" Journal of Value Inquiry, Vol. 9 (1975), 303-306.

Holmes, Robert L. "Frankena on 'Ought' and 'Is.'" The Monist, Vol. 64 (1981), 394-405.

Hume, David. A Treatise of Human Nature (1739-40). Ed. L.A. Selby-Bigge. Oxford: Clarendon Press, 1888.

Jager, Ronald. "Analyticity and Necessity in Moore's Early Work." Journal of the History of Philosophy, Vol. 7 (1969), 441-458.

Jaggar, Alison M. Feminist Politics and Human Nature. Totowa, NJ: Rowman and Allanheld (div. of Littlefield, Adams and Co.), 1983.

James, William. "The Sentiment of Rationality" (1882) and "What Makes a Life Significant" (1899). Both repr. in John J. McDermott (ed.). The Writings of William James (2nd ed). Chicago: University of Chicago Press, 1977, 317-345, 645-660.

Johnstone, Henry Webb, Jr. Philosophy and Argument. University Park, PA: Pennsylvania State University Press, 1959.

Klemke, Elmer Daniel. The Epistemology of G.E. Moore. Evanston, IL: Northwestern University Press, 1969, cited as (1969B).

Koehler, Wolfgang. The Place of Value in a World of Facts. New York: Liveright, 1938 (see esp. Chapter III, "An Analysis of Requiredness," 59-87, and Chapter IX, "Facts and Forces," 150-280).

Korsgaard, Christine M. "Two Distinctions in Goodness." Philosophical Review, Vol. 92 (1983), 169-195.

Kovesi, Julius. "Principia Ethica Re-Examined: The Ethics of a Proto-Logical Atomism." Philosophy, Vol. 59 (1984), 157-170.

Lear, Jonathan. Aristotle and Logical Theory. Cambridge: Cambridge University Press, 1980.

Levi, Albert William. Philosophy As Social Expression. Chicago: University of Chicago Press, 1974 (see Chapter 5, "Contemporary Philosophy. The Age of the Professionals: G.E. Moore," 233-300).

Levy, Paul. Moore: G.E. Moore and the Cambridge Apostles. New York: Holt, Rinehart and Winston, 1979.

Lewis, Clarence Irving. *An Analysis of Knowlege and Valuation*. La Salle, IL: Open Court Publishing Co., 1946.

———. *Values and Imperatives*. Ed. John F. Lange. Stanford, CA: Stanford University Press, 1969.

Lewy, Casimir. "G.E. Moore on the Naturalistic Fallacy." *Proceedings of the Brith Academy*, Vol. 50 (1964). Repr. in Ambrose and Lazerowitz (eds.), *G.E. Moore: Essays in Retrospect* (1970) (q.v. above, under Broad), 292-303.

MacIntyre, Alsdair. *After Virtue*, (2nd ed.). Notre Dame, IN: Notre Dame University Press, 1984.

Masterman, Margaret. "The Nature of a Paradigm." In Imre Lakatos and Allen Musgrave (eds.), *Criticism and the Growth of Knowledge*. London: Cambridge University Press, 1970, 59-89.

McCloskey, Herbert J. *Mata-Ethics and Normative Ethics*. The Hague: Martinus Nijhoff, 1969.

Merleau-Ponty, Maurice. *The Invisible and the Invisible*. Ed. Claude Lefort, Trans. Alphonso Lingis. Evanston, IL: Northwestern University Press, 1968 (see esp. Ch. 4, "The Intertwining-The Chiasm," pp. 130-155).

Midgley, Mary. *Heart and Mind: The Varieties of Moral Experience*. New York: St. Martin's Press, 1981.

Miller, Richard W. *Analyzing Marx: Morality, Power and History*. Princeton, NJ: Princeton University Press, 1984.

Mitroff, Ian. *The Subjective Side of Science. A Philosophical Inquiry Into the Psychology of the Apollo Moon Scientists*. New York: American Elsevier, 1974.

Moore, G.E. *Principia Ethica*. Cambridge: Cambridge University Press, 1903. Rev.ed. 1922, abbr.as PE.

———. *Ethics* (1912). New ed., London: Oxford University Press, 1947. Repr. 1965, abbr. as E.

———. "The Conception of Intrinsic Value." In *Philosophical Studies*. New York: Harcourt Brace, 1922, 251-274, abbr. as CIV.

_____. "Is Goodness a Quality?" (1932). Repr. in *Philosophical Papers*. London: Allen and Unwin, 1959, 89-100, abbr. as PP.

_____. "Reply to My Critics." In Paul A. Schilpp (ed.), *The Philosophy of G.E. Moore* (1942) (rev. ed). La Salle, IL: Open Court Publishing Company, 1968 (esp. 535-627), abbr. as PGEM.

Moritz, Manfred. "The Naturalistic Fallacy and Its Different Forms" (trans. Dru Ritezel). In John William Davis (ed), *Value and Valuation: Axiological Studies in Honor of Robert S. Hartman*. Knoxville, TN: University of Tennessee Press, 1981.

Murdoch, Iris. *The Sovereignty of Good*. New York: Schocken Books, 1971.

Najder, Z. *Values and Evaluations*. Oxford: Clarendon Press, 1975.

Neville, Robert. *Reconstruction of Thinking*. Albany, NY: State University of New York Press, 1981.

Nozick, Robert. *Philosophical Explanations*. Cambridge, MA: Harvard University Press, 1981.

O'Connor, David. *The Metaphysics of G.E. Moore*. Dordrecht and Boston: D. Reidel Publishing Company, 1982 (Philosophical Studies Series in Philosophy, Vol. 25).

Olthius, James H. *Facts, Values and Ethics: A Confrontation With 20th Century British Moral Philosophy, in Particular G.E. Moore*. Assen: Van Gorcum, Ltd., 1968.

Orenduff, J.M. "Hume, Moore, and Naturalistic Ethics." *Journal of Value Inquiry*, Vol. 14 (1980), 157-161.

Orwell, George. *A Clergyman's Daughter*. New York: Harcourt, Brace, 1935.

Pastin, Mark. "The Reconstruction of Value." *Canadian Journal of Philosophy*, Vol. 11 (1975), 375-393.

Peirce, Charles Sanders. Collected Papers of Charles Sanders Peirce. Ed. Charles Hartshorne, Paul Weiss and Arthur W. Burks (8 Vols.). Cambridge, MA: Harvard University Press, 1931-1935, 1958.

Pielke, Robert G. You Say You Want a Revolution: Rock Music in American Culture. Chicago: Nelson-Hall, 1986.

Popper, Karl R. The Open Society and Its Enemies (Vol. II, 5th rev. ed). Princeton, NJ: Princeton University Press, 1966 (1st publication, 1945).

_____. "Replies To My Critics." In The Philosophy of Karl Popper (q.v. under Schilpp), Vol. Ii, 961-1197.

Prior, Arthur N. Logic and the Basis of Ethics. Oxford: Clarendon Press, 1949.

Putnam, Hilary. Realism and Reason (Philosophical Papers, Vol. 3). Cambridge: Cambridge University Press, 1983 (see esp. Chapter 16, "Beyond Historicism," 287-303).

_____. Reason, Truth and History. Cambridge: Cambridge University Press, 1981 (see esp. Chapter 7, "Fact and value," 127-149).

Regan, Tom. "Moore's Accounts of 'Right.'" Dialogue (Canada), Vol. 11 (1972), 48-58.

_____. "Moore's Use of Butler's Maxim." Journal of Value Inquiry, Vol. 16 (1982), 153-160.

Rescher, Nicholas. Introduction to Value Theory. Englewood Cliffs, NJ: Prentice-Hall, 1969.

_____. Methodological Pragmatism: A Systems-Theoretic Approach to the Theory of Knowledge. New York: New York University (NYU) Press, 1977.

_____. The Strife of Systems: An Essay on the Grounds and Implications of Philosophical Diversity. Pittsburgh: University of Pittsburgh Press, 1985.

Roberts, H.W. "Some Queries Suggested by G.E. Moore's Beautiful and Ugly Worlds." Journal of Philosophy, Vol. 38 (1941), 623-627.

Robinson, Richard. *Definition*. Oxford: Clarendon Press, 1954.

Rohatyn, Dennis A. "Aristotle and the Limits of Philosophic Proof." *Nature and System*, Vol. 4 (1982), 77-86 (cited as (1982A)).

_____. "Burying Moore's Naturalistic Fallacy." *ACPA Proceedings* (Houston, TX), Vol. 56 (1982), 173-185.

_____. "Moore After Eighty Years: Analysis, Common Sense, and the Role of Philosophy." *History of Philosophy Quartery*, Vol. 3 (1986), 207-225.

_____. "Moore's Damage Report." *Journal of the British Society for Phenomenology*, Vol. 13 (1982), 193-194 (cited as (1982B)).

_____. *Naturalism and Deontology: An Essay on the Problems of Ethics*. The Hague: Mouton and Company, 1976.

Sarkar, Shukla. *Epistemology and Ethics of G.E. Moore. A Critical Evaluation*. Atlantic Highlands, NJ: Humanities Press, 1981.

Sartre, Jean-Paul. *Being and Nothingness: An Essay in Phenomenological Ontology* (1943) (trans. Hazel E. Barnes, abridged ed.). New York: Citadel, 1964.

Schilpp, Paul A. (ed). *The Philosophy of Karl Popper* (Library of Living Philosophers), 2 Vols. La Salle, IL: Open Court Publishing Company, 1974.

Scott, Robert B., Jr. "Five Types of Ethical Naturalism." *American Philosphical Quarterly*, Vol. 17 (1980), 261-270.

Searle, John R. *Speech Acts: An Essay in the Philosophy of Language*. Cambridge: Cambridge University Press, 1969.

Shrader-Frechette, Kristin S. *Nuclear Power and Public Policy. The Social and Ethical Problems of Fission Technology*. Dordrecht and Boston: D. Reidel Publishing Company, 1980 (see esp. Chapter 6, "Nuclear Safety and the Naturalistic Fallacy," 135-167).

_____. Science Policy, Ethics, and Economic Methodology. Some Problems of Technology Assessment and Environmental-Impact Analysis. Dordrecht, Boston and Lancaster: D. Reidel Publishing Company, 1983 (see esp. Chapter 3, "The Retreat From Ethical Analysis," 67-105).

Smith, Anthony. The Politics of Information. Problems of Policy in Modern Media. London: Macmillan, 1978.

Snare, Frank. "Three Sceptical Theses in Ethics." American Philosophical Quarterly, Vol. 14 (1977), 129-136.

Soghoian, Richard J. The Ethics of G.E. Moore and David Hume: The Treatise as a Response to Moore's Refutation of Ethical Naturalism. Washington, DC: University Press of America, 1979.

Stout, Jeffrey. The Flight From Authority. Religion, Morality and the Quest for Autonomy. Notre Dame: University of Notre Dame Press, 1981 (see Chapter 9, "Beyond Metaethics," 179-200).

Strawson, Peter Frederick. The Bounds of Sense: An Essay on Kant's Critique of Pure Reason. London: Methuen, 1966.

Turner, Stephen P., and Regis A. Factor. Max Weber and the Dispute Over Reason and Value: A Study in Philosophy, Ethics, and Politics. (International Library of Sociology). London: Routledge and Kegan Paul, 1984.

Walton, Douglas N., and Lynn M. Batten. "Games, Graphs and Circular Arguments." Logique et Analyse, Vol. 27, No. 106 (June 1984), 133-164.

Weber, Max. The Methodology of the Social Sciences (trans. Edward A. Shils and Henry A. Finch; Foreword Shils). New York: Free Press, 1949 [see esp. "The Meaning of 'Ethical Neutrality' in Sociology and Economics" (1-47) and "'Objectivity' in Social Science and Social Policy" (49-112)].

_____. "Politics As a Vocation," and "Science as a Vocation." Both repr. in *From Max Weber: Essays in Sociology* (trans. and ed. Hans H. Gerth and C. Wright Mills). New York: Oxford University Press, 1946, 77-128, 129-156.

White, Alan R. *G.E. Moore: A Critical Exposition*. Oxford: Basil Blackwell, 1958 (see esp. Chapter VII, "Ethics," 117-147).

Willis, Paul. *Learning to Labor: How Working Class Kids Get Working Class Jobs*, 2nd ed. New York: Columbia University Press, 1981.

Winner, Langdon. *Autonomous Technology: Technics Out-Of-Control as a Theme in Political Thought*. Cambridge, MA: MIT Press, 1977.